THE
COFFIN
CONFESSOR

THE
COFFIN
CONFESSOR

THE
COFFIN
CONFESSOR

SOME
LAST WISHES
DON'T GO
QUIETLY
TO THE
GRAVE

BILL
EDGAR

PENGUIN BOOKS

PENGUIN BOOKS

UK | USA | Canada | Ireland | Australia
India | New Zealand | South Africa | China

Penguin Books is part of the Penguin Random House group of companies
whose addresses can be found at global.penguinrandomhouse.com

Penguin
Random House
Australia

First published by Penguin Books in 2021

Cover design by Adam Laszczuk © Penguin Random House Australia Pty Ltd
Front cover images courtesy Getty Images (grave) and Stocksy (sky)
Back cover author photograph courtesy Newspix/Glenn Hampson
Internal design and typesetting by Midland Typesetters, Australia

Printed and bound in Australia by Griffin Press, part of Ovato, an accredited
ISO AS/NZS 14001 Environmental Management Systems printer

A catalogue record for this
book is available from the
NATIONAL
LIBRARY
OF AUSTRALIA
National Library of Australia

ISBN 978 1 76104 295 9

penguin.com.au

MIX
Paper from
responsible sources
FSC
www.fsc.org
FSC® C009448

For Lara

Contents

1

It's your funeral

It was a perfect day for a funeral. A bright summer morning on the Gold Coast. In a few hours the heat and humidity would skyrocket, baking the steepled roof until the chapel was oven hot. But for now the weather was on the side of the mourners, who shuffled into the church to pay their respects to the deceased. The men wore simple black suits, the women tasteful knee-length dresses in muted tones, with the occasional splash of colour.

I filed in along with them, sombre, head bowed respectfully while we took our seats, chairs scraping and shoes squeaking.

The ceremony opened with a few words from the priest, a hymn, and then a big fellow seated in the pews stood up and slowly made his way to the lectern. There, he stood for a moment, shuffling the papers he'd prepared for the eulogy. He introduced himself as John, the best friend of Graham, the deceased, and welcomed us to his farewell. They'd all known and loved Graham, and they'd all miss him.

John was a big guy – the silver-haired, red-faced Queensland farmer type used to getting his own way. The sort of man who wore a big, easy smile on his face as he made his way through the world. But his mouth turned down as he cast a sad look towards the coffin that held his best friend in the whole world, Graham Anderson.

John stared off into the chapel mournfully, took a deep breath, then began to speak. The crowd listened respectfully as he delivered his opening words. His voice echoed through the chapel, over the sound of gentle weeping from some of the mourners. It was a beautiful scene, a Hollywood-perfect opening to a funeral service.

After exactly two minutes had passed, as arranged, I stood, tugged my suit vest down to neaten it, and cleared my throat. I reached into my vest pocket to retrieve a letter.

'Excuse me, but I'm going to need you to sit down, shut up, or fuck off. The man in the box has a few things to say.'

Every eye in the room turned to me. The priest's jaw hit the floor. He didn't know what was happening – he was in shock, by the looks of things. But my attention was focused on John. He was the one I had come to confront, and I kept an eye on the would-be eulogist while reading from the letter, which Graham had given me.

By the way the colour drained from John's face, I could tell he knew what this was about. He was shit-scared. As well he should have been.

I'll explain why in a moment, but first we'll have to go back in time a few months, back to when I first met Graham, the man lying in the coffin. He'd hired me as a private investigator.

* * *

Being a private investigator – or PI if you're short on time – is pretty much what it says on the tin: my clients hire me to investigate things that someone else would prefer to remain private. If you believe the way we're portrayed in the books, films and the media, you'd think most of that work is following cheating spouses around with a telephoto lens camera. And you'd be right.

A huge percentage of PI work is just men and women who have grown suspicious of their significant other and want someone to bring them evidence that confirms that suspicion. There are whole agencies dedicated to this line of work. They'll hang around and stalk your spouse until they can bring you the unhappy proof that they are running around on you.

That was never my forte, nor was it something I particularly enjoyed doing. The way I see it, if you're so suspicious of your partner that you're prepared to hire a PI, then I can guarantee your marriage has problems. I'll save you some cash by telling you what you already know: they're screwing around, and you'd be better off hiring a marriage counsellor than a PI.

Apart from infidelity, nearly every other job involves looking into some kind of commercial problem for the client. Theft, fraud, blackmail. In the end, most PI work comes down to money. Love and money – the only two things that get your average person worked up enough to call a PI.

Graham's case involved a little of both. He first engaged me in early 2016 to investigate his finances. A farmer in his mid-sixties, Graham was a self-made man. But he'd recently fallen ill, and had been unable to keep up with the workload of managing his business. He had a suspicion that, while he was laid low, his accountant was taking advantage of his reduced faculties. He'd noticed a little money going missing here and there, and things weren't quite adding up; he had a gut feeling that someone was ripping him off.

Graham reached out to me because I have certain skills in that area, but I couldn't take the job straight away because I was flat out with other work. But Graham wanted my skill-set in particular, and he was happy to wait.

When I was finally available to investigate properly, about half a year later, I worked out what was going on fairly quickly. Money *was* being funnelled from his accounts, and I was able to figure out by whom. With enough pressure applied to the accountants in question, the money was returned and the case was closed. Graham considered it a good result.

Sadly, that's where the good news ended for Graham. He was in worse health than he'd let on, and at the conclusion of my investigation, as we were wrapping up, he disclosed that he was terminally ill. He'd been happy to wait the six months it took for me to take the case on because he thought he had plenty of time. That turned out not to be the case.

'I thought I had longer than this,' he told me, as I sat by the bed he could no longer leave. 'But I suppose everyone thinks that. You get told you've got just a few months to live and you think, *Oh yeah, whatever, I feel great, I'm going to live for years.* I didn't know it was all going to go this fast.'

Our conversation led to matters of mortality – death, the afterlife. Graham wasn't really afraid of dying, but he was curious about what happens to us after we close our eyes that final time.

'I don't have any idea what'll go on after I'm gone, or where I'm going to end up, but wouldn't it be nice to know?'

'Well, let me know once you find out,' I said. 'Send some sign from the other side. Let me know if you enjoyed your funeral.'

He shook his head. 'I don't reckon I will. I already know I'm going to hate my funeral.'

Graham told me that he didn't think much of most of the funerals he'd been to. He was always surprised and disappointed, because he'd expect to see a true reflection of his loved one in the memorial service – the things that made them unique, that people loved them for. The good *and* the bad. Instead, he got a sanitised, watered-down picture of some kind of saint, delivered by a priest that nine out of ten times didn't know the deceased from a bar of soap. He'd even had friends who had recorded their own video eulogies, only for their message to be considered inappropriate for some reason, and the service instead ran a slideshow of photos from their life.

Graham mentioned that he'd like to write his own eulogy. He'd fill it with the things that really mattered to him, leaving the world in a way that he felt actually represented the way he'd lived.

'Why don't you do that?' I said. 'Film a video and get them to run it at the service.'

'I know they would never run it. Someone would decide it was too confronting for my family and friends, and they'd be afraid of insulting those left behind. There's no point.'

'I could always do it for you,' I joked. 'Crash your funeral and deliver the eulogy that you really want.'

We had a laugh about it, shook hands, and said goodbye. I didn't give it another thought.

But a few weeks later I received a call from Graham.

'I've been thinking,' he said down the line. 'I'm going to take you up on that offer.'

'What offer?'

'I want you to crash my funeral. Interrupt the service and read out the message I'm going to write for you.'

'Are you serious?'

'Dead serious. And I'm going to pay you ten grand to do it.'

Fuck me, I thought. 'That's a lot of money.'

'There's a lot I want to say. You see, there's something I want revealed at my funeral. My best mate, John, is insisting on giving the eulogy.'

'So? What's wrong with that?'

'He's also trying to screw my wife.'

* * *

It turned out that Graham had an important bit of personal business to settle before he could rest in peace. John, his best mate of many years, had been trying to crack on to his wife.

In fact, pretty much from the moment Graham got ill, old mate John had been secretly trying to get into Mrs Graham's pants. Even though she hated the bloke! She wanted nothing to do with him, and hadn't approved of the friendship for years. But for months now, John had been cornering her in her home, trying to kiss her, patting her on the bum, putting the hard word on her. At first she didn't tell Graham, because she didn't want to upset him, but in the end she didn't know what else to do about it.

But once she told him, Graham didn't know what to do about it either. He was your typical country bloke – in his younger years, he had been a very hard man, doing what he needed to in order to get by in the world. There's a certain kind of man, particularly from that place and time, who is used to settling things with fists, and has no skills in verbal confrontation. Graham had worked hard, paid his way, done all the right things in life. But now here he was, sick and dying, unable to deal with this betrayal directly.

Even if he did confront old mate John, Graham knew his friend wouldn't give a shit – harassing your dying friend's wife isn't the action of a man who feels shame.

So Graham wanted me to interrupt the service at his funeral, where John had already volunteered to do the eulogy, and put him to rights in front of all the people they knew, something Graham didn't have the strength to do anymore.

'I feel weak,' he confessed. 'I hate it, being so helpless. I'm ashamed that I can't do anything about it.'

He felt awful about what he could see going on, and I did too. It was obscene for a man on his deathbed to be watching someone he'd trusted sexually harassing his wife, unable to intervene. Graham clearly loved his wife with all his heart – it was quite cool, to see this hard man not afraid to have a soft side – but it also meant that what his mate was doing really hurt him.

I thought to myself, if my mate did that to me, I'd be gutted. Imagine being called upon to defend your family and you're too sick to do it – you can't move, you can't act. It's just a shocking dilemma. That's probably why I refuse to have close friends.

Anyway, that's what convinced me to take the job. Graham's situation really got to me. Certain events in my own life have given me sympathy for anyone who finds themself helpless and at the mercy of those they thought they could trust.

'You're on,' I told Graham. 'Fuck that guy. I'll crash your funeral service and tell him how it's going to be.'

'Do you think that's out of line?'

'It's up to you,' I said. 'It's your funeral.'

* * *

While my instinct was to help a dying man out, at the same time I couldn't just take Graham's word for it. I needed proof.

If there's one thing I've learned as a PI, it's that there are three sides to every story: yours, theirs and the truth. Experience has taught me not to trust anyone or anything until I have evidence – and there's always a way to get that.

With Graham's permission, I set up a hidden camera inside his home. That sort of thing is illegal, unless you have the permission of the homeowner, in which case anything goes. At the start of my career, something like that would have been a huge procedure – installing the cameras, recording everything, retrieving the footage – but spy camera technology is so advanced these days, it makes everything a lot easier.

You can get these tiny little cameras that take up almost no room, and they upload the footage straight to the cloud, so it can be accessed from anywhere. You can have cameras hidden inside stuffed toys to keep an eye on nannies, or cameras hidden inside lipsticks to catch cheating husbands. You can go online and buy a body camera that looks exactly like all the other buttons on your shirt. The moral of the story is: in today's world, you can never be too paranoid.

Setting up the camera in Graham's house was straightforward. I used a little camera, not much bigger than a thumbnail, and placed it on his bedhead. That let me see straight down into his hall and into the kitchen and dining area. It was where Graham had advised me to put the camera to get the most footage, and it was essentially the view from his deathbed. I got a front-row seat to everything he saw.

It wasn't pretty. By the next evening, I had all the proof I needed.

Pretty much the second John thought he was alone with Graham's wife, he was moving in on her. Patting her behind, trying to kiss her neck. He'd try to grab her in the hallway as she passed and she'd have to push him away. Real sleazy eighties-movie bullshit. He'd spill a drink on his shirt on purpose and then take it off and ask her to wash it for him, and then he'd be standing there flexing his muscles. What a fucking wanker.

One look and I could see from his behaviour that this was not the first time John had tried it on. Like Graham said, this had been going on for months.

I went to Graham with the footage, but it was nothing new to him. That's why he'd hired me to crash his funeral. The situation was pretty dire. I had no hesitation at all.

Not long after that, Graham passed away. The time from when he first disclosed to me how ill he was and his passing was only a matter of weeks, and it had been just nine days between me agreeing to crash his funeral and Graham drawing his final breath. By then, everything had been settled. My client had made a deathbed request of me, and nothing was going to stop me from following through.

* * *

On the day of the funeral, the hardest part was knowing what to wear. Not a lot makes me nervous. I live on the fringes of the Gold Coast, close to both an army base and a tropical rainforest. Depending on the season, I'm dealing with snakes, spiders, cyclones, floods, bushfires. And that's just at home. As a private investigator, I'm used to all sorts: criminals, cops, drugs addicts, liars, thieves, extortionists. None of it bothers me. For a long time, getting punched in the face was my idea of a good time.

But before Graham's funeral, I was hugely concerned about picking the right outfit. It seemed pivotal and I got absolutely stuck on it, as though I was a debutante on the way to my first ball. Should I wear black? Black is the colour of mourning, but I wasn't exactly a mourner. In the end, I decided on a suit without a jacket – trousers, white shirt, tailored vest. It was nice, respectful attire, but without being too over the top.

So, all dressed up, I entered the church, and had one final moment of indecision: where should I sit? Traditionally the pews on the left-hand side of the church are for family, and those on the right are for friends. I wasn't family, but I wasn't really a friend, either. I didn't actually know anybody there.

For my part, I had been trying to fly under the radar, saying nice stuff about Graham when I was spoken to, but not drawing attention to myself. But as I was walking into the church, people came up to me and paid their respects.

'I'm sorry for your loss,' they said, or, 'How did you know Graham?'

I could only give a vague answer. 'We used to work together.'

Which was true, after all. He'd hired me and I was there to do a job.

In the end, I chose to sit with the family, near enough to the front to do what I had to do.

When John stood up and took to the podium, I identified him easily. He started to give his speech – a hypocritical, dishonest, self-serving recounting of the life of his dead friend. Graham had instructed me to interrupt his best mate's speech no less than two minutes in, so that was when I got to my feet and made my introduction.

'Excuse me, but I'm going to need you to sit down, shut up, or fuck off. The man in the box has a few things to say. My name's Bill Edgar and I'm here on behalf of the deceased, who has a message for you all.'

The church was so quiet that you could hear the rustle of the paper echoing through the corners of the hall. I unfolded Graham's final message and read aloud.

'John, it's Graham Robertson here. I've hired Bill to interrupt your eulogy to tell you that I witnessed you, on several occasions, trying to screw my wife. God love her, she rejected every one of your advances. But that doesn't change the fact that a mate does not do that. Especially when one is lying on his deathbed. I hate you for what you did, and what you were trying to do. My final wish is that you fuck off from here. You're not welcome at my funeral, and you're certainly not going to speak on my behalf.'

I looked up from the letter. John had dropped his notes – I heard them fall to the floor in the hushed room. He was gripping the sides of the lectern and his face had turned a really funny colour. He must have been paler than my poor client in the box. That was great to see.

You could tell this turn of events had knocked the wind right out of him, which I wasn't unhappy about either. The guy had a really punchable face. Imagine Bob Katter without the hat – silver hair, red neck, a really cocky, king-shit-of-a-small-town vibe.

Before I was done, the dude lost his nerve and left, full of shame. A woman, who I assume was old mate's wife, got up and followed him out. She looked furious.

A few others in the congregation tried to object, telling me to sit down, but I calmly told them the man in the box had more to say.

'Either you stay and listen to what that is or you too can fuck off,' I said politely, and kept reading from Graham's letter.

'Further, if my brother, his wife and their daughter are here, you can kindly fuck off too. I haven't seen you in thirty years, and now you show up to pay your respects? You never respected me in life, so why should you respect me now? Where were you when I was alive and could have used you around in the hard times?

'This funeral is for my loved ones, who I will miss dearly, and for my wife, who I loved until my last breath. I love you still.'

With that, I folded up the letter, put it back in the envelope, and walked up to the casket, where I laid it gently on the wood.

There was still not a sound in the church as I walked back down the aisle, my footsteps ringing out behind me until I reached the double doors.

If the service continued after I left, I don't know. That wasn't really my business. I'd kept my promise to my client and delivered on his final wish to dish out some measure of justice to his best mate, who'd revealed his true colours the second Graham was too sick to defend himself.

I was on my way to my car when a young woman called out to me. She caught up with me and introduced herself as Graham's daughter. She thanked me for what I'd done.

'Dad would have loved that,' she said. 'And Mum loved it too. I'm so happy this happened.'

She told me that her mum had not known what she was going to do about John, especially now that Graham was gone, as he'd kept coming on to her again and again even after she'd let him know he disgusted her. Now that the guy had been shamed in front of his whole community, her mum didn't think she needed to worry about him ever again. Even better, that community knew she'd knocked him back at every step, and her own reputation was secure.

'Happy to help,' I said, and I was.

My whole life up to that point had made me into the kind of bloke who does not give a fuck about what people think of him. There are a few things I do care about: my wife, my kids, and those who can't look after themselves. After all – if we can't trust those closest to us, what chance do we have in life?

2

Commissioned estate

In my childhood we lived in many rental homes, and seemed to move quite a lot. At times there were eleven of us all living together in one house – me, my grandparents, my aunt and uncles, my mum, my brother and sisters, all crammed into three bedrooms, usually with only one bathroom between us. It was hard to get along with everyone under the one roof, and fights often broke out, verbal or otherwise.

I have vivid memories of that time. None more so than when the police were called to the house we were renting and kicked us out into the street. All the grown-ups and kids just sitting in the street, surrounded by the few possessions we had. With so many of us living in the one house, you'd be forgiven for questioning why the meagre rent wasn't able to be paid.

One of my uncle's friends was a tow-truck driver, and he came and collected the lot of us, allowing us to stay in a caravan on a spare block of land.

The first house I remember living in – an actual home, not a caravan or the floor of a friend's rental unit, or a donga by the side of the road – was given to us by the government. It was meant to put an end to our life of moving from house to unit to caravan to street.

Mum had been on the waiting list for quite some time, and finally, when I was eleven years old, she was given a community house in a commissioned estate. Everything about it was new: a new building, on a new street, in a new neighbourhood.

I couldn't believe our luck. It was beautiful. The only way I could understand our good fortune was that we must have won the lottery. Looking back now, that house had been built fast, cheap and shoddy – everything was made of fibro and plastic. But I remember running through the rooms, relishing the feeling of the wooden floorboards under my bare feet, and out into an actual backyard. The first backyard I'd ever had. There was nothing in it yet – no lawn, no landscaping, just dirt and concrete. But you can build on dirt and concrete, and I was already full of plans for the place. I'd be out there digging holes, starting a proper garden, searching the neighbourhood for trees that I could dig up and replant. It's a really nice memory, how excited I was. I guess I was trying to make a home for us. I was just a kid, but I could tell this was a new start, a proper chance at life, and with me as the man of the house.

The entire estate had been built for down-on-their-luck families. Refugees, immigrants, drunks and drug addicts. And my mum.

I guess every home has issues. There's good and bad in every family. In our case, Mum had more than her fair share of the bad. My mum wasn't an alcoholic, and she didn't do drugs – except for Bex, the three-in-one tranquilliser, stimulant and anti-depressant. Half of her generation, particularly housewives, was addicted to Bex, because it was available over the counter, handed out like lollies. Just as doctors handed out Ritalin to us kids with behavioural patterns that baffled them.

But the addiction Mum did have was just as destructive – to herself and to our family. She was a gambler. She had it real bad. Any spare minute, any spare dollar: down to the pokies and straight into the slot machines.

We lived in Queensland, where slot machines weren't widely available, but we were right on the border with New South Wales, so she'd just jump across the state line to gamble. No matter what else was going on in our lives, she'd always find her way there. She did whatever it took to get her to the pokies: public transport, a lift with a friend or driving herself – when she had a car.

Mum loved her cars, and the freedom they represented, with all her heart. Her favourite was an aqua-coloured Austin that Mum called Maude. At least while she had it. Every once in a while there'd suddenly be a car parked in our driveway, seemingly out of nowhere – but only until she needed to get some quick cash to gamble, and then the next day the car would be gone again.

One week we'd have a house full of furniture and appliances – comfy sofas, a nice TV, a fridge packed with food. The next week it'd all vanish, everything we owned in the hock shop. We'd be sleeping on the floor with empty stomachs. Then, two weeks later, she'd have a big win, and suddenly we had food to eat again.

It was a pretty fucked way to build a life, but the memory of that house remains beautiful to me. So much so that, every now and then, I drive over there and sit outside the old place, remembering the good times. Until the memories of the bad times flood in, that is. Then it's time to go.

We were so happy to be there – everyone in the neighbourhood was. All of us on a brand-new commission housing site, getting a second chance at life. In time, of course, that faded. The shiny and new estate quickly became run-down, and it grew rougher by the day. In those areas, you really have to be strong to survive. That or you just stay locked up indoors, never going outside. Or, when it all gets too hard, you pack up and move.

That's what ended up happening to Mum. We were there for maybe four years. Then she couldn't make the meagre rent payments and we had to go.

But that house was a window into a life I'd never thought existed. Prior to that I'd never been exposed to that level of security and safety. A roof over my head, food on the table. Since I could remember, Mum had never worked a day in her life, and yet she was given a house to live in. Even more unbelievably, she had still fucked it up.

That realisation, while bitter, was sort of a catalyst for me. I wanted to prove that I could do better. This will always be in the back of my mind: never forget where you came from. Never go back, never look back. Most importantly, use every experience, good or bad, as fuel for a better future.

* * *

Out of everyone in the family, only my grandfather was able to hold down a job. He worked behind the counter at a local corner store, and on the weekends he delivered groceries to those who couldn't come into the shop for themselves. The income from this job made him the de facto boss of the family, and he relished his role as the patriarch. He held the purse strings, and nothing in the family happened without his say-so.

When I was approaching eight years of age, Grandad asked me if I wanted to work with him behind the counter after school and on Saturday mornings. I was thrilled at the offer – it would mean serving sweets to children, and not only would I make two dollars a week, I would have access to all the lollies I could stomach.

Grandad told my mum it would help me to learn maths, and that I would soon become very good at addition and subtraction. I recall Mum exchanging a look with him before nodding and giving her approval.

I was stoked. We only lived a few blocks away from the store, so I would get up early and ride my bike there. The only rule, as with most kids those days, was to make sure I was home by the time the street lights came on. I made sure that I was, because to be late would mean a solid beating.

For months afterwards, I worked at the corner store every day. Up at dawn, home at dusk. At the end of the week Grandad would give me the two dollars, and when I got home Mum would take them from me. 'For safe-keeping.'

True to her word, she kept the money so safe that I never saw a cent of it. Not unless I could steal it back before it went into the pokies.

* * *

On the rare Saturdays when I wasn't needed at the store, I went to soccer practice. I was a gun soccer player – it was just something that clicked for me the first time I set foot on a soccer field. Every minute I could, I spent practising, and getting better and better.

I really did have a gift for the sport. From the first game I played, I was better than most of the other kids in terms of technical ability, and I was faster than even the best of them. All without proper gear – I would play barefoot, rocketing up and down the field.

It wasn't until I was ten years old that I got a chance to join a real soccer club, Surfers Paradise Soccer Club. I was told to turn up for my first training session in white shorts and a blue t-shirt, like all the other kids. I still had no boots, so I came barefoot, while most of the other kids had shiny, studded soccer boots. I was still faster than them.

I impressed the coach, and he predicted, 'You'll play for Australia,' tousling my hair.

The coach was the father of one of the other boys, and he was a great bloke. He would bring a big bag of oranges to the training sessions and games. Because food was scarce at home, I would always eat as many as I could, stuffing orange after orange into my face. The coach had to tell me to slow down, promising that I could take some oranges with me to eat on the way home.

At the start of the season each child was given a permission slip for their parents to sign, to be returned with the fees for the club's ground and equipment hire. I'd given it to Mum, but she neglected to pay or return the form.

One afternoon, just two weeks out from the first game, the coach pulled me aside and told me that, without permission from my mum, he couldn't let me play.

'Mum is coming to see me train next time,' I promised. 'She'll give you the fees then.'

She had said she would be there, and I'd honestly thought she would turn up. She never did.

But a father of one of the other boys in the team stepped in to pay my fees, and even bought me my first pair of soccer boots. They were beautiful: black rubber and leather, with a blue cat racing down each side. Although the leather was very hard, the boots were super comfortable and fitted me perfectly. When I first wore them at training, I was able to kick the ball harder and further than ever before.

I was thrilled. I never wanted to take them off! I even rode my bike home still wearing them, and then raced inside to tell Mum what had happened. She seemed happy for me, and while she had no money to pay for my soccer training, it was nice that someone else cared enough to give me the chance.

Grandad, however, was not as happy for me. In fact, he was furious. He accused me of stealing the boots, or of begging someone to buy them for me. I denied both accusations, which only made him angrier. He flung open the front door and threw my new boots out into the street.

That upset my mum, and she tearfully tried to defend me. A vicious fight broke out between the two, both of them screaming bloody murder. When they finally stopped arguing, Mum looked as though she wanted to slap me across the face. I retreated to my room.

It felt horrible that all this yelling was all over me – that this was my fault. That night I leapt out of my bedroom window to retrieve my boots and bike, and I rode away into the night. This was the first of many times I ran away from home.

That first runaway attempt didn't last long. I guess I'd expected my mother to come looking for me, but she knew I had nowhere else to go and would return eventually. After only an hour on the run, I came home, still wearing my new boots, which I'd forgotten to take off again.

Mum opened the front door. She told me that Grandad wanted to see me. He was waiting for me in his bedroom.

To get to my grandparents' bedroom I had to pass the living room, where my brother and sisters were watching television; they paid no attention, eyes glued to the screen. I swung open the door of Grandad's bedroom and, sure enough, he was sitting on his bed, his black leather belt wrapped around his knuckles.

'Get inside,' he told me. 'And touch your toes.'

I was in tears – trembling at the sight of the belt – long before the first blow.

That first strike, when it came, was staggeringly powerful, catching me across the backside. I stumbled and quickly straightened, rubbing my bottom, only to be struck again, my fingers taking most of the second blow. The third was across my calves, which forced me to the floor, where Grandad continued to strike me across the legs.

I curled up as tight as I could, crying for help. It went on and on.

Eventually Mum came into the room.

'He's had enough,' she told Grandad, telling me to go have a bath and get ready for bed.

As I ran the bath I could hear another argument breaking out between the rest of the family. Again, I knew it was over me, and that this would not be the end of it.

Very upset, angry, and in a great deal of pain, I stood on tippy-toes to examine my legs and bottom in the bathroom mirror. Angry welts were already rising from the skin, which then turned itchy in the warm water of the bath.

That night I lay awake on the top bunk, which I shared with my brother, who had the bottom, trying not to scratch at the welts. The door swung open, and Mum came in to ask that I go and say sorry to Grandad before he went to bed. I climbed down from the bunk bed, still wiping away tears, and entered the lounge room, where Grandad was watching television.

'I'm sorry,' I said.

'Come here.' He picked me up and sat me on his knee.

He held me very tightly, pushing me into his chest, while the light from the television flickered over me. For a long time we sat there, and both Mum and Nanna walked past, commenting on how cute I looked sitting there. They did not notice, apparently, the fear in my eyes, or the way I was shaking, as Grandad held me more and more tightly.

* * *

My first game with my new soccer club was postponed. It had rained so heavily the night before that the field was too soaked to play on. Mum suggested that, instead, I help Grandad out at the store. I didn't mind, because Grandad would let me eat lollies – 'our little secret' – and play the pinball machine.

It was an unusually quiet day, and Grandad was boxing groceries and running them out to his car boot, to be delivered to customers on his way home. I sat at the lolly counter while he bustled about. A typical Saturday in every way.

Then he came in, leaned against the counter and, after a moment, patted me on the knee.

'I saw you touching yourself last night,' he said.

I had no idea what he meant and looked at him, baffled.

'You heard what I said,' he told me in a low voice. 'You were playing with yourself. I caught you.'

'Did not!' I protested. 'You're a liar!'

Grandad slapped me across the face. The blow came without warning, and it was so hard I tumbled off the stool, catching my lip on the lolly counter as I fell.

I lay on the floor for a moment, tasting blood. Grandad knelt by my side and handed me his handkerchief, suddenly concerned. He told me not to worry, that it was only a graze, but that I should be careful to never speak to him that way again, because there would be consequences.

Just then, the little bell on the door rang. A customer entered the shop to buy his morning paper. When he saw the blood running down my face, he asked, 'What happened to you? Are you alright?'

I wanted to scream and run away, but Grandad told the man I was fine. I had been swinging on the stool instead of working hard, but I would be okay.

'Well, that'll teach ya,' said the customer.

He grinned, picked up his paper and walked out. The little bell on the door rang as it shut, leaving me alone with Grandad again.

The shop had a bathroom and toilet out the back, and Grandad told me to go out there to clean myself up. If anyone asked what happened, I was to say I fell off the stool while misbehaving. If I didn't, I would be in terrible trouble.

That day I was scared to go straight home, so I rode to a little cubbyhouse I had made, in a hiding-hole behind a local motel called the Pink Poodle. It was a cosy place where I could eat my lollies and pretend I was in a home of my own, away from my family. It was a place where I could feel safe, because only I knew where it was.

I stayed out as late as I dared, and by the time I got home the street lights had already been on for ten minutes. When I got home, I knew I was going to cop it.

Mum looked at my fat lip and told me she had been worried sick, and so had Grandad, as he had told me to go straight home after leaving the shop. They'd feared I had been snatched by a stranger. She told me that as part of my punishment I was going to miss out on playing soccer the next Saturday too, and instead go work with Grandad at the store again.

By the next weekend my lip had healed, and I had put the previous Saturday's events behind me, thinking it was all over. Just like the previous week, I sat quietly behind the lolly counter while Grandad packed the car with groceries. And just like the previous week, when he was done he came and looked at me strangely.

'Have you thought about what I asked you last week?'

'No,' I said, looking at the ground. I didn't understand, and didn't want to think about it.

'You have so,' he said. 'Have you been playing with yourself?'

I had no idea what he meant, or what I was supposed to say. Above all, I was terrified of another slap, so I whispered, 'Yes.'

That seemed to please him. 'Show me what you do,' he told me. 'When you play with yourself.'

25

I was shaking now, trembling with fear. I placed my hands on my lap and slowly started to rub my upper thighs, thinking maybe this was what he wanted me to do, but that only frustrated him. He reached down and grabbed my private part and squeezed. He held me there in a vice-like grip, so hard that blinding pain shot up and down my spine. He talked to me in a very calm voice, telling me that I was not to say anything to anyone about our little talks or what we did in private.

'Do you understand?' he asked. 'Do you promise?'

I immediately said I did, hoping that would make him release his grip. After a minute, he did. I made my escape.

For days afterwards I was sore, especially when I tried to go to the toilet. I found it hard to pee, and would often have to sit on the loo instead of standing, as the effort and pain of peeing became unbearable. I would have to sit there, crying silently, in pain as I tried to pass urine. I could not ask to see a doctor, because I could not for one second stand the idea of someone finding out what had happened to me. It was far too embarrassing. Nor could I ever dream of asking for help with what Grandad was doing.

* * *

A few days after my birthday that year, a new bike was waiting for me out the front of the house. It was lime green with black wheels and silver spokes – heaps bigger and fancier than my old bike. I loved the new bike, and Mum was thrilled that I was so excited. She told me that Grandad was going to take me down to a park he knew, where they'd installed a bike track, so I could ride it around and get used to it.

My excitement quickly turned to fear. I'd figured out by then that I was only safe around Grandad when someone else was with us, and today it would just be the two of us, alone in the park.

During the drive, Grandad kept up a steady stream of conversation – how was soccer, was I enjoying school, was I making many friends? They were normal questions, and I gave normal answers. It seemed like a regular conversation between a child and a grown-up. Slowly, I began to relax. Maybe it was over?

On arriving at the park, Grandad hauled the new bike out of the boot of the car and walked with me as I wheeled it to the gates. A concrete pathway – done up to look like a racing track – led out into the parklands, past a duck pond where waterbirds of all types had made their homes. Elsewhere in the park barbecues, tables and chairs were set up for family picnics, and children raced around play equipment and swing sets. Large concrete footprints had been poured at intervals, to make it look like a giant had walked through the park, and children were playing at jumping from footprint to footprint. At the far end of the park a river snaked through the greenery, full of kids splashing about or sitting on blow-up mattresses. Basically an idyllic scene for a kid my age, and I immediately fell in love with the park, which I decided to call 'Big Foot Park' after the giant concrete footprints.

In another life, with another family, it would have been a wonderful day.

Grandad instructed me to go for a ride while he sat at one of the park benches. I raced around the pathway several times, picking up speed as I grew more comfortable with the bike, until Grandad called me over to eat. He'd brought a can of soft drink and a bag of potato crisps for me. While I ate, Grandad handed me a white paper bag. I opened it and pulled out a pair of blue and red swimmers in my size.

'Put them on. Then you can go and join the other kids and go for a swim,' he said.

I looked around – we were surrounded by other people, including kids my age. The thought of my peers seeing me without pants on was mortifying, and so I asked if I could go to the toilet to change. He told me no, that I was to get changed here where he could keep an eye on me. I was a little scared, but more embarrassed that some of the other kids might see me.

I changed by shimmying out of my shorts until they fell to my ankles, leaving my shirt and underwear on to protect my modesty. It was a slow, awkward process and Grandad told me to hurry up. He leaned towards me, forcibly yanking my underwear down and helping me to pull up my new swimmers. He seemed pleased with them, and happy for me to join the other kids in the river having fun.

I had only just dived into the water when my grandad waved me back to the park bench and told me it was time to head home. There was no towel, so Grandad passed me my shirt to put on over my still-wet torso. I went to grab my shorts, but Grandad had already packed them up and started walking back to the car. He put my shorts in the boot, along with my shoes and the bike. Dripping wet, I moved to retrieve my shorts, but Grandad slammed the boot shut, nearly taking my hand off.

'You stupid boy.' He clipped me over the ear, which stung quite a bit, then dragged me to the passenger side of the car and opened my door, waiting for me to climb in.

The drive home was quiet. No more questions about school or my friends. Finally, he broke the terrible silence.

'Did you like the park?'

'Yes.'

'Did you have a good time?'

'Yes.'

'Have you been playing with yourself?'

I started to tremble.

'What's the matter?' Grandad asked. 'Are you cold?'

Before I could answer, he placed his hand on my right leg and started rubbing it up and down as though to warm me up. With each stroke, he touched my wet swimming trunks.

'Do you like what I'm doing?' he asked. 'Does that feel good?'

Shaking uncontrollably now, I was unable to answer, which seemed to anger him terribly. He pulled the car over to the side of the road, leaned towards me and pulled my hair so hard that tears came flooding to my eyes. He told me I was being disrespectful and needed to be taught a lesson. I quickly told him that I was sorry and that I didn't mean to be naughty.

His mood changed again, quickly, and he told me that he loved me and that I was his favourite. That he cared for me and that anytime he asked if I liked something he was doing I was to say 'yes' in a loud and happy voice.

Placing his hand on my swimmers he again asked if I liked what he was doing.

'Yes,' I replied.

'Do you want me to do this to you all of the time?'

Again, I said, 'Yes.' But there were tears streaming down my face. His hand immediately moved from my swimmers to give me a quick slap across the face.

'There,' he said. 'Now you've got something to cry about.'

From that day on, my Grandad abused me every chance he had. He always asked me the same disturbing questions, then proceeded to put his hands where I most hated them.

After he had finished, he would grab me by the hair or the back of my neck, and he would squeeze so tight that my eyes would start to water. In hindsight, I know that it was because he was disgusted with himself for what he was doing to me, and had to find a way to justify it to himself. That I liked it, or that I was in some way responsible, and so he had to punish me for that. He had to find a way to live with himself. That's why he hated it when I cried.

Afterwards, when I was alone, when he couldn't hurt me anymore, I cried as much as I could.

* * *

Early one morning, I was watching television. It was a children's show and it featured a talking puppet called Agro, who I thought was incredibly funny. I loved the way he talked back to adults. If I ever tried that, I would have been beaten half to death.

The show often had a guest on, a policeman in a neat uniform who was called 'Officer Dave'. He warned the children that talking to strangers could be dangerous. It turned out that's not where the danger in my life was coming from.

I was watching the show when Mum came in and told me she had a surprise for me: Grandad was taking me fishing. I looked at her, confused for a moment. I protested that I didn't feel well and that I didn't want to go fishing with Grandad. She became angry, and told me that I was an ungrateful little sod. I should be grateful Grandad was going to spend time with me and teach me how to fish.

'It will make him happy,' she said. 'So you should make an effort to be happy too. Smile for your grandad.'

Grandad's boat was his pride and joy – a mustard-coloured half-cabin with a black Mercury motor on the back. He'd go out on the ocean and go fishing, or kill time by cruising up and down the Broadwater, an estuary just north of Surfers Paradise. That's where we were going that day – to a boat ramp near where we lived, then off across the Broadwater.

On the way to the ramp, Grandad asked me if I'd ever been fishing. I told him that me and a friend sometimes went to the river and threw a net in, but that we'd never caught anything but a half-dead toadfish.

'That's not fishing,' Grandad said, laughing. 'I'm going to teach you how to fish for real.'

As we were motoring across the Broadwater, Grandad asked if I would like to drive. Of course I said yes. I'd never driven a boat before, but Grandad showed me how to steer and operate it, even though I could barely see over the prow. It was so much fun – hitting the throttle and feeling the boat accelerate across the water.

Grandad pointed to a small island in the middle of the Broadwater and told me to head towards it. That's where we would drop anchor, as he reckoned the fish would be biting around that area.

Sure enough, when we got there the water was clear as glass and the sandy floor of the Broadwater only looked ankle deep.

I could see schools of tiny fish swimming under the boat and figured we were about to catch heaps.

As Grandad was getting everything ready, he told me to remove my shorts, shoes and socks.

'Why?' I asked.

'It'll make it easier to move around the outside of the cabin. And you'll be able to swim to safety if you fall in.'

This seemed to make sense, and the morning was hot and sunny, so I stripped down to my underwear.

Grandad had the rods and reels ready, and he showed me how to bait a hook and then cast my line out as far as I could. Each time I started to reel my line in, he would snap at me.

'Wait! Have patience. The fish aren't dumb – they all swim in schools. You have to catch the one that's running late. The lazy one that's always looking for a meal.'

Suddenly my fishing rod started to jiggle and bend. I had caught my first fish! Excited, I started to reel it in. But Grandad seized the fishing rod from my grip, and he reeled in the fish a lot faster than I could have managed.

'Grab the net,' he told me, and I scrambled to grab the fishing net and scoop the fish up out of the water.

'It's a whiting,' Grandad announced once he got a look at it. 'Quite a big one too!'

I was overjoyed. I'd caught a fish! My very first fish!

Grandad showed me how to take the fish off the hook and place it into a bucket half filled with water.

As he baited the hook once again, and cast out my line, I looked at the fish in the bucket staring back at me. Suddenly I didn't feel so happy about my catch. It looked so sad and lonely, and I felt so sorry for it that I decided I wouldn't mind if I never caught another fish.

As the morning passed, I periodically checked on the fish in the bucket, making sure it was alright. The sun overhead grew hotter and hotter, and I moved the bucket into the shade. Meanwhile, Grandad was getting frustrated, as he couldn't get a bite. He suggested we move to a new location. But first, he asked if I wanted to go for a swim.

It was boiling hot by now, and a swim to cool off sounded nice, but I didn't want to leave the fish alone on the boat. I knew that if I told him I felt sorry for the fish, Grandad would think less of me, so I told him I didn't feel like swimming, but refused to explain why.

This made him sigh deeply. Changing topics, he asked me if I knew what the front and rear of a boat was called, then explained that the front was called the bow and the rear the stern.

I found this very funny – why didn't they just call it the front and back? Grandad didn't know, but to make me prove I now understood the difference between the bow and the stern, he told me to go stand at the stern, which I did. I balanced there precariously for a moment, then in one quick movement Grandad came up and threw me into the ocean.

The water was deeper and colder than it had looked from the boat, and panic took over. I started thrashing and screaming.

Grandad was furious. He reached over the side of the boat and grabbed me by the arm, dragging me towards the ladder onto the deck. He held me there in a vice-like grip.

'You can only come back on board if you like me playing with you,' he said. 'Tell me that you like it.'

I didn't say anything. I was too scared and upset to get any words out at all. The water was cold, but the shock of it had made me realise I was already badly sunburned.

Grandad grew impatient. He dragged me up the ladder himself, then pushed me into the cabin.

'Take off your clothes and dry yourself with a towel,' he ordered.

After I had dried off, he asked me to hand him my clothes and towel, which he hung up to dry over the boat's rail. Naked, embarrassed and ashamed, I started to cry. Grandad told me to go and sit at the front of the boat – as he couldn't stand the sight of me crying.

The place he wanted me to sit was unbearably hot – the fibre-glass had been under the blazing Queensland sun for hours. My skin sizzled when I tried to sit down, but when I stood back up Grandad was furious.

'Sit down!' he roared. 'Or I'll give you something to really cry about.'

This scared me enough that I sat back down, putting my hands under my bottom so I could shield myself from the worst of the heat. Even this was excruciatingly painful.

For the rest of the day I sat on my hands while the sun beat down on me. Grandad fished alone. I was not allowed to throw a line in again, and Grandad caught nothing except the whiting we had caught together.

I felt terrible for that fish. From my spot on the bow I could see the sun beating down on the bucket it was kept in. I knew that no matter how awful I felt in the sun, the fish must feel worse.

Eventually I asked if we could throw it back, but Grandad said no.

'I'm going to show you what happens to lazy fish that only think of their bellies and are late for school.' He grabbed the fish from the bucket and produced a long filleting knife. Holding the fish down against the boat as it struggled, he looked me right in the eye. 'It's the same thing that happens to little boys who tell lies.'

He stabbed the fish in the belly and slid the knife up towards its head. Then he pushed his fingers inside the fish and pulled its guts out while it was still alive. The moment it stopped struggling, he threw the fish, and the guts, back in the water.

I tried not to let him see how upset I was, but he knew. He told me to always remember what happened to that fish if I ever thought about telling anyone what he did to me. Then he made me sit on his lap naked, all the way back across the Broadwater and back to the boat ramp.

By the time I got home, the skin across my back and shoulders had turned an angry red, and was terribly painful to lie on.

After a few days the sunburn blistered and peeled, but the skin on my bottom – where I'd been forced to sit on the hot fibreglass – had suffered a different, deeper burn. Those burns became infected, and my underwear would get stuck to them, ripping small bits of skin off every time I changed clothes, and the wounds would then start to bleed. It took forever to heal, and I was in incredible pain for weeks afterwards.

I never wanted to go fishing again, and hated the thought of going out on Grandad's boat. Whenever the idea came up I would throw such a tantrum that my mother grounded me, banning me from going outside or doing anything fun. I was fine with that, because that included fishing trips with Grandad.

Mum, for her part, hated my tantrums. But I was a child, desperately afraid, deeply in need of her attention and protection. I wanted nothing more than to wrap my arms around her and tell her what was going on, but I felt there was never the right opportunity. She always seemed to have more important issues than mine: finding money for rent, for gambling, or for the Bex that she took, having long lie-downs on the couch during her daily headaches.

The longer the abuse went on, the dirtier I felt, scared and upset with myself for not being able to make it stop. The more upset I became with myself, the more it seemed to disgust my mother.

One day she overheard me telling my sister that I hated Grandad, which set off an uncontrollable rage in her. She beat me and berated me; I was ungrateful, I didn't appreciate everything Grandad did to keep our family together.

'After all he has done for you, this is how you treat him!' She ripped the power cord off the kettle to make a whip. 'You ungrateful little bastard.'

She hit me over the back of the legs with it, again and again, leaving welts across my legs and bum that burned and itched. They, too, seemed to take forever to heal.

Once she had calmed down, she held me close and admonished me more gently. She explained that Grandad was a good man, and that we all had to do our best to show our gratitude.

One time, and one time only, I tried to confide in my nanna. I approached her while she was preparing dinner for Grandad, who was outside in his shed, bottling his home-brew. She was running a block of cheese over a box grater. I gathered my nerve and decided to come right out with it.

'Nanna,' I said. 'Grandad is hurting me.'

She stopped. I remember clearly the sound of the cheese grater stopping, and then blinding pain. She'd turned, her face twisted in rage, and struck me with the grater. She caught me across the shoulder blades, right below my neck, and thrashed me with it until my upper back was latticed with tiny little cuts. I was helpless, shocked and in tears.

All of a sudden she stopped. She wrapped her arms around me, and I realised she was sobbing herself.

She gave me a huge cuddle – the biggest I'd had in my life – and told me that if Grandad hurt me it was my fault. If I wasn't naughty then he wouldn't have to punish me. She said she was sorry, but I had to start trying harder to be a good boy.

The welts on my legs were agonising, and they slowed me down, but they were nothing compared to the tiny cuts from that cheese grater. They became badly infected – nasty little scabs – and they were a reminder to keep my mouth shut and never confide in anyone.

To this day, I can't look at a cheese grater. But the worst part is remembering how sweet that hug was. No one had ever hugged me that way before, showed me any real love. That was the closest I'd come in my whole short life.

It would be years before I saw what it was like to grow up with a mother who loved you, who protected you from harm. But by then a whole lifetime had gone by.

3

What's in a name?

A week after Graham's funeral, I received a message from a stranger on Facebook – a young lady who'd been at Graham's funeral. She wanted me to visit her aunt, Christine Chambers. Christine was dying, and on hearing about the incident at Graham's funeral, she'd told her family she wanted to engage my services to interrupt her own funeral.

I agreed to meet with her, but to be honest, I was a little surprised. When Graham asked me to crash his funeral, it had seemed like a one-of-a-kind sort of request; one fed-up guy who'd hit upon a solution to the very specific problem of his sleazy, so-called best friend.

So when someone else got in touch within a week, asking me to interrupt another funeral, it struck me as more than a coincidence. It got me thinking that maybe there was something here. Maybe this was something people needed – a way to reclaim some agency over how our deaths are marked, the way we're remembered.

The more I thought about it, the more it made sense. How many funerals had I been to where the service was actually an honest reflection of the person in the casket? Barely any. Some of the most fun-loving, eccentric characters I've known – people who were absolutely brimming with life – were remembered with a series of sanitised platitudes, delivered between a tame slideshow and someone pressing play on 'Wind Beneath My Wings'.

Most of the time, the eulogy was delivered by some priest who barely knew the deceased, instead making up the speech as they went along. I found it excruciating – some dude in robes reading off his cue-cards like he's a schoolboy trying to cheat his way through a book report. Fuck that.

I've always been allergic to hypocrisy and bullshit, but especially when religion comes into it. Who wants their dead body carted into the church of a God they barely believed in while they were alive, in order to be eulogised by a total stranger? Why is this very specific ritual imposed on everybody by default? In Australia, we're meant to be a secular society. It's your right to believe in any divinity or spirituality that suits you, or to reject the idea entirely.

What is it about funerals that makes them sacred, beyond any criticism? It's not as though our Western idea of funerals was handed down by a man on a cloud; it's a ritual that has evolved over centuries. It started in the Dark Ages, when we buried our dead under piles of rocks to stop them being dug up by wolves!

Even the modern palaver is not that recent, so why should one size fit all?

Throughout history there have been a thousand different ceremonies that societies have thought of as the only proper way to mark the passing of a loved one. Cultures that built funeral pyres and threw your ashes in a river. Cultures that pushed you out to sea on a boat and shot you with arrows. Cultures that threw your body off a cliff. Cultures that pulled your guts out through your nose, wrapped you in bandages and built a pyramid on top of you.

I realised that what I was about to start would be confronting and controversial, but so unique that it would gain the attention of the world. That's when I decided I needed a name for this kind of work. Not just any name, but one that sent a clear message: 'I'm here, and like me or loathe me, you won't forget me.'

The service I would provide to the dying was granting them one last wish, a way for the powerless to leave the world with their conscience clear and the slate wiped clean. A confession before the coffin. The Coffin Confessor.

The Coffin Confessor identity would be my way of lending my voice to the departed.

The way I see it, people have a right to shuffle off this mortal coil in whatever way they'd like. Everyone should be able to be as true to themselves in death as they were in life. I would make it my job to tell the people my clients loved how much they were loved, and to tell those they hated to fuck off.

* * *

Christine was unique. Just a beautiful soul. I liked her from the very first moment I met her. She was elderly, very weak, but still embodied this really old-school sense of class. A real lady:

charming, elegant and kind. It was like Mary Poppins had walked off the screen and into suburban Australia.

Our first meeting was supposed to be short and business-like, but I ended up staying for hours, just drinking cups of tea and listening to her stories. She'd had a full life, travelled all over the world – a trip to Egypt as a little girl, back when it was still occupied by Britain, and later on holidays with her children and grandchildren.

In the end I spent three days with her. Longer than I needed to, really, but it was very easy to spend time with her and her family. The dynamic of her family made a real impression on me – Christine exuded love for everyone around her. I kept thinking to myself what a caring person she was, and how wonderfully that care was reflected back to her. She'd built this little world of adoration all around her.

I looked at her and thought, *Fuck, I wish she'd been my mum. I wish I'd been a part of this family*. What a difference it would have made to my life. What a mother she must have been – it would have been amazing to grow up in the orbit of this woman.

The flip side, of course, was how much it hurt her to be taken away from her family. It's an inevitable fact – one day we die, and on that day we'll have to say goodbye to our loved ones – but it seemed so unfair that it would happen to Christine.

It gutted me, to be honest. Seeing such a wonderful woman suffering. And I couldn't do anything to help her with the pain.

She had leukaemia, and it was tearing her apart from the inside. There wasn't much time left – a few months, at best. She'd had every possible procedure to delay the inevitable; lung surgery, and a spinal tap, which is an awfully painful procedure.

She'd been through some incredible suffering, but still, she was brave and kept smiling through it.

Her husband, Derick, was an absolute fucking mess at the thought of losing her. He was a neat man, an engineer, who had always been able to find solutions to problems throughout his life. But he knew this one would evade him, and it terrified him.

I think it was a bit of a relief for him once I was on the scene, because the poor guy couldn't manage it. He was dropping shit, spilling his tea, bursting into tears. A great guy, but utterly ruined. He couldn't imagine life without his wife. I understood – it had only been three days but *I* could barely imagine life without her.

Christine wasn't scared of dying, but she was angry. Just royally pissed off that she was being called away from the life she'd built, and furious at the idea that it was inevitable.

That's something I was struck by. *Yes*, I thought, *you should be fucking angry*. Fucking oath, you're dying, and you look around and see you've got so much to live for, but it's all being ripped away from you.

Christine was religious – Catholic – and active in her church. She had a strong belief in the afterlife, and that gave her some comfort, knowing she would see her family again in heaven.

Part of her belief meant that she was surrounded by angels – they comforted her in life, and would do so after death. She would talk to them when she was alone or afraid, as well as during prayer. All her life she used the angels to talk to loved ones who'd passed away. She believed that it helped them stay alive in a way, and helped their memory live on.

'After I die, talk to me as much as you can,' Christine told me. 'I'll be listening.'

I had no doubt that she would be remembered, living on in people's memory. She would be leaving a huge hole in the world, but she was content. She was dying as happily as anyone could hope to.

Christine was full of love, and that was part of the problem, really. That's why she had hired me.

Christine didn't have a grudge against the world. There was no score to be settled, no enemy she needed confronted, no figure in the chapel who had wronged her. No, Christine's regret was someone she loved. Someone who wasn't her husband. Her lifelong best friend, Carol.

'What were we supposed to do?' she asked me sadly. 'It wasn't right for a woman to be like that in our day – in the sixties and seventies.'

I understood. It was hard enough for men back then – they could live closeted lives as 'confirmed bachelors' – but women were expected to marry, raise families, do all the right things. It was unimaginable.

If Christine and Carol were born today, things would probably be different – open marriages, polyamorous relationships, there are all sorts of options. But half a century ago they had just been two women with a shared secret they could never tell even each other.

Some people can be in love with two people at the same time and never act on it. It's never happened to me, but it can happen to anyone, and it's what had happened to Christine.

* * *

The funeral was lovely; really very touching. I wasn't there to disrupt the proceedings or confront anyone, and it proved to be a beautiful, respectful service.

When the time came, during a pause between the priest's message of love and the eulogy, I stood up and gently cleared my throat.

'Excuse me. My name is Bill Edgar and I am the Coffin Confessor. I'm here on behalf of my client Christine Chambers, who lies before you.'

I opened the envelope and read aloud.

'To my husband, Derick. I love you with all my heart. Please don't be sad. We will meet again, but until then live life, enjoy what you have – God knows life is short. I'll be taking the memories we made together with me. I love you, and thank you for being there for me. I'm no longer in pain, and I hope your pain will ease knowing that I'm okay. I love you, my darling.

'To my children and grandchildren, I wish I could have watched you all grow up and become the beautiful people I know you will be. I will miss you, but I will be watching over you. Please never forget me and talk to me as often as you can. I'll be listening. I love you all. God bless.'

I paused for a second. The mood in the church was sombre but respectful. Nobody had been expecting me to pop up and interrupt, but nobody had a problem with it. It was clear that everyone in the room loved Christine and was happy to hear from her one more time. I looked back down to finish her final message.

'And finally, to my closest and best friend, Carol. I love you. Thank you for your love and support, not just for me but my family. Please know that, if life had been different, I believe we would have been more than just friends. You are my inspiration, and I'm sorry that we couldn't be together in this life. Derick, put your tongue back in your mouth. Thank you all for being here. I love you.'

And with that I sealed the letter again and sat down.

Normally, after crashing a funeral, I leave the letter on the coffin and simply walk out, but this time it seemed appropriate to stay a while. The congregation were lovely. Afterwards, several of the gathered mourners thanked me for the final message from Christine and invited me to the wake. I declined politely – that seemed beyond the realm of what I'd been hired for.

It turned out that Christine's declaration of secret love was not too much of a shock to anyone. Everyone who'd loved her knew about the special bond she'd shared with Carol, although they didn't know exactly how deep the feelings had gone.

Christine had asked me to quietly disclose to Carol just how much she'd wanted to be with her. Apparently, Carol had always sort of known, and always felt the same way. They'd even had a moment where they'd come close to disclosing how they felt about each other, but had never acted on it.

Carol, like Christine, seemed sad that they'd never found a way. They'd both had long lives, loving husbands, families – but they'd been in love with each other the whole time. It must have been a kind of torture.

There was nothing about Carol that read as queer to me, but I've learned not to judge a book by its cover. We shook hands, I passed on my condolences once more, and then I left.

Pretty sad, that one. It didn't fully hit me until long after the funeral itself how profoundly Chrisine would be missed. I still think about her, the remarkable life she'd led.

Now and again, I'll talk to her, as she asked me to do. She was a rare, genuinely wonderful person, and people like that deserve to be remembered and to be remembered the way they really were. The way she'd lived. With love.

4

Love me not

Mum didn't love me the way a mum is supposed to love her child. She didn't even love me as much as she loved my sister or my younger brothers.

I was the second eldest, but the only child that reminded my mother of my father. She hated him and, as I grew older, she made it clear that she hated me too, because every time she looked at me I reminded her that he existed.

She even made me go by a different name, just so that she wouldn't associate me with my dad. His name was William (Billy) Edgar, so one day she insisted I call myself Scott Robinson, Scott being my middle name and Robinson her maiden name. She banned me and everyone else from referring to me as William. If I kept calling myself Will or Bill, that would mean a beating. So I became Scott.

For the first few years of my life, I thought that's just what families were like. Erratic, filled with endless fighting and constant neglect, punctuated by emotional abuse. My first real insight into what a family could be didn't happen until I was eleven, when I met my childhood best friend, Michael.

The new government home had opened up for us and suddenly we had a place of our own, away from our extended family. Just Mum, my brother and sisters, and me.

It was in another suburb, which meant changing schools in the middle of the year. This somehow made it necessary for me to repeat Grade Six, but it was a small price to pay to live further away from my grandad.

Plus the new school was nowhere near as rough as the previous one. It was a public school that catered to an area of the Gold Coast that spanned both the comfortable upper-class waterfront areas and the more rough-and-tumble outer suburbs, including the housing estate where I lived. So the school was a strange mixture – dirt-poor kids like me, but also wealthy kids destined for private high schools.

One of those turned out to be the best friend I would ever have. Michael loved sports just as much as I did, and he was as close as I'd ever come to an equal on the soccer field. We met on the playground and became friends pretty much instantly.

At that age, I had no idea about the distinctions and divides between poor and privileged children, and we did the same sorts of things as all the kids in the neighbourhood. We'd race each other down at the bike tracks, hang out at the skate bowl, or just play out on the street for hours and hours until the sun went down and the street lights came on.

One day Michael asked me if I wanted to come over to his house and play tennis.

'I'd love to,' I said, even though I had never been to his house, wasn't quite sure what tennis was, had never seen a court, and had no idea how to play.

The next Saturday, I woke up early and rode out to the BMX track, where Michael would meet me and then take me to his house. We rode along the footpath of a tree-lined street until we came upon a gleaming black driveway. It must have been 40 metres from the road to the house itself, which was the biggest in the neighbourhood. Honestly, my first thought was that Michael must have lived in a motel. I just could not get my head around the idea of a private home that spectacular.

My idea of a house was a two-bedroom prefab with three generations crammed into it. But this house had separate bedrooms for each family member, and spare rooms for guests on top of that. The five-car garage alone was bigger than our place. Our backyard was a stretch of dirt fenced in by cheap palings – Michael's had a pool and a full-size tennis court.

'Let's have a hit,' Michael said. He took me around to the court and handed me a tennis racquet.

I'd never held a tennis racquet before, so I just watched what Michael did and imitated his swing. On the first try I smashed it back and caught him by surprise. Then again. Ball after ball, I landed my return right where I had to in order to win the point.

Michael was taken aback.

'You told me you'd never played before!'

'I never have. Honest!'

It was funny watching him get more and more frustrated as the game went on, but I was telling the truth. The game just made sense to me, the same way all sports did. It didn't matter what it was, if you gave me a few minutes to get the hang of it, I was good at any sport. That's just where my talents lay, I guess.

Michael loved sports even more than I did, especially soccer, but also skiing. Skiing didn't seem to me like a particularly good sport to pursue in sub-tropical Queensland, but the wealth his family possessed let him spend all his holidays on snowfields – driving all over Australia, or jetting off internationally.

Michael had everything a boy could want and more. The best of everything: toys, TVs, clothes. He was always well dressed, and always had the latest must-have items.

He had never known what it was like to live without and, looking back, he probably didn't have the life experience to understand that this type of privilege was not something all kids grew up with. He was exceptionally generous with all his stuff – his parents would buy him a new bike and he'd give me his old one. I couldn't believe it – this incredible BMX racer, a little smaller than his new one but practically still brand new, and he was just giving it away.

His mum and dad were just as kind to me. They treated me like one of their own, welcoming me into their home, letting me stay the night, feeding me proper meals with meat and vegetables. Michael's family ate at a dinner table, with good cutlery, in a cheerful, mood-lit dining room. It was surreal to me, like walking into a family off the TV.

The time I spent with Michael's family was one of the only times I remember in my whole childhood where I felt safe. The life he lived was like a different planet to the one I returned to after my visits.

One time I tried to tell Michael what happened to me at home. I'd never confided in anyone before. When the abuse started,

I was shit-scared that if I told anyone it would get back to Grandad. Then it became embarrassing that it had been going on so long, and that shame was added to the fear. Michael was the first person I thought I might be able to trust with the truth.

I remember asking him, just one random afternoon while we were out riding our bikes, if his grandad ever touched him.

'What?' He looked shocked. 'No! What do you mean? Touch me? Does your grandad touch you? What are you saying?'

Instantly I became defensive. 'No, of course not. It's just something I heard on TV. Ha!'

I never brought it up again.

* * *

I was twelve years old, playing soccer, when I noticed a man on the side of the field was watching me closely. My life experience so far had made me suspicious of strangers, especially middle-aged men watching young boys play soccer, so I was wary when after the game he approached and complimented me on my talent on the field. He asked if I'd ever thought of trying out for a school scholarship.

'What's that?' I asked him, which seemed to surprise him.

'Well, it means you get to go to a special kind of school. For special boys.'

The school he had in mind was the Southport School, a well-regarded Anglican private school for boys, known as TSS for short. It's the kind of place that calls its graduates 'old boys' rather than 'former students'.

I still didn't really understand what the recruiter meant, but I liked the idea of being selected to attend a school for only a special type of boy. Another thing I didn't understand then was that most of the boys at that school weren't actually all that special, beyond being born into obscene wealth.

But I recognised the name of the school. It was where Michael and some of the other boys in my year would be going when they graduated primary school. The idea of going to the same school as Michael sounded great to me – I was more than happy to take home the envelope the man gave me and pass it on to my mother for her to read, sign and return, which she did.

Later that year, Mum was contacted by the same man who'd approached me on the soccer field. He invited us both to an interview for me to receive a place at the school on a full scholarship. I was very happy, but Mum was a little reserved. We still had no money, and she was acutely aware of that fact. She shopped exclusively in charity stores, and got around in overalls or jeans and a t-shirt. Despite this, my mother took a lot of pride in her appearance, and she tried to look her best no matter the occasion.

I remember arriving at the school and feeling like I was landing in another world. I'd never seen anything like it outside of a movie. In my mind, a school was a few long corridors alongside a field of grass, with maybe a few demountable classrooms if you were lucky. At Southport it was turn-of-the-century imperial brick buildings with steepled roofs, arched columns and arcade walkways.

The long driveway was lined with looming trees, and I caught glimpses of manicured lawns and sporting grounds as far as the eye could see: soccer fields, yes, but also ovals for cricket and football, basketball courts, a pool, a gym, sheds for sailing and rowing. My entire experience with organised sports up until then had been

playing in parks and on public ovals, which were always either dry
and scuffed up or muddy and scuffed up.

As we approached the cluster of elegant buildings, we drove
under the shadow of a looming gothic revival clock tower, the
biggest clock I'd ever seen. Mum explained that it was a minia-
ture replica of Big Ben, the famous clock tower at Parliament in
London. As we climbed out of our car and walked up the pristine
footpath towards reception, the clock began to chime. It was one
of the most beautiful sounds I had ever heard. In the coming
years I'd often wait around in the clock's shadow, waiting for it to
chime, just to hear that sound.

The path to reception took us past a large Anglican-style
church, set amidst lovingly tended gardens with beautiful flowers
in every colour of the rainbow and lush green grass. I had absolutely no frame of reference for what I was seeing – I could only
imagine this was how Charlie had felt the moment he stepped
through the doors of Willy Wonka's chocolate factory.

Inside, we were greeted by two boys dressed in what I at first
took to be business suits: blue shirts, grey trousers, navy blue
blazers and polished black shoes. As I would soon find out, this
was the formal school uniform, which was worn on special occasions. These polite, confident young men were students of TSS.

They escorted my mother and me to a dining room lit by
stained-glass windows three storeys high. There we found tea,
coffee and biscuits laid out on a long white table, and the boys
asked us what refreshments we might like.

My mum ordered a coffee for herself and an orange juice for
me. The juice arrived refreshingly cold, and while I sipped it the
young men showed us around the room. The building we were in

was built in 1901 and formed part of the clock tower. We spent a few minutes admiring the stained glass, art and photographs of the school's sporting champions – people who had gone on to represent Australia or win medals at the Olympics.

Eventually an older, distinguished man in an elegant suit entered the room. He introduced himself as the school's headmaster, shook my mother's hand and gave me a quick pat on the head, messing up the hair that my mother had spent half the morning fussing over.

We followed him to his office, which was so large, and had such high ceilings, that his voice echoed as he spoke. It sounded as though the room were empty, although it was beautifully furnished with antique desks, stuffed chairs, lamps and artworks.

'I must congratulate you on becoming one of the finalists of the bursary scholarship,' he told me, speaking at great length about the school and its proud sporting achievements. He was sure I would fit in very well with the sporting community, as he had heard about my skills on the soccer field.

He turned to my mother and explained the details of the scholarship on offer. What would be needed to qualify, and what it would entail.

Then, as quick as it had started, it seemed the interview was over. I was sure we had failed somehow. Judging by the way he stood up briskly and thanked us for coming, we must have made some mistake. He told us to expect an answer by post in the coming weeks, and that seemed to confirm we were not part of his plan.

As he led us out to the grand hallway, he suggested that we might like to take a look around the school. He volunteered one of the students to escort us around and answer any questions we may have had. I was excited at the prospect of seeing more of the school, but my mother declined the invitation. We quickly made to leave.

On the way back to the car we passed two younger boys, around my age, both wearing dress suits. I realised that these boys were my competition for the scholarship. When I asked Mum about this, she grew angry.

'Only posh boys get to go to a school like this,' she said. 'That's definitely not you. People like us don't belong here. I should never have brought you here in the first place.'

The thought that I would see this school and not be allowed to attend it was very upsetting. I asked if she could send me to the school without the scholarship. The look she gave me cut through me like a knife.

'Are you stupid?' she demanded. 'Do you have any idea how much it would cost to go to a school like this? Don't be daft.'

On the drive home I was so upset I could have cried. I felt even worse when I noticed my mother had tears of humiliation running down her face. She looked hurt, ashamed and angry all at once. I vividly remember telling her that it was okay, that I didn't really want to go to a school that had all boys and no girls.

I was disappointed, of course, but by the time we got home I had abandoned all hope of the scholarship. I put it out of my mind.

* * *

Normally, the postman rode his bike to the mailbox in front of our house, popped the letters in and went on his way. But one morning, in December 1979, he dismounted, walked up the driveway, and hand-delivered a large yellow envelope to Mum.

I'd been playing backyard cricket with my brother, so I came over and watched nervously as Mum sat down on the porch steps with the letter. My understanding of envelopes that size and colour was that they meant someone in the family was in trouble with the law or that we'd have to move house again.

Mum called out to me, asking me to join her on the steps.

'Do you know what this is?' She waved the envelope in front of me, showing me the TSS logo.

That's when I realised that this envelope contained the answer I had been waiting for. Suddenly I could barely contain my excitement. Mum reminded me to not get my hopes up, and made me promise I wouldn't get upset when I learned I'd failed.

I gave her my word, so she shrugged and opened the envelope. She pulled out a thick stack of correspondence, it must have been fifty pages, all neatly printed and stapled. It took me a moment to make out the first word on the first page, but that was all I needed to know. It said: 'Congratulations.'

This was a word my mother had never said to me, but I'd heard it from other parents and my soccer coach. It meant you had done well and achieved something. It couldn't mean anything bad – it only ever meant good things. I had won the scholarship. I would be going to TSS, one of the finest schools in the country, along with the rest of the 'special' boys.

All the details were outlined in the document, along with the steps that needed to be taken to ensure I was ready for my first class. I had been granted a bursary scholarship for five years, which meant all expenses were paid except for uniforms, books and excursions.

Before school was due to begin, Mum took me down to the uniform shop, where she was horrified to learn that the uniform – second-hand shoes, socks, shorts, two shirts and a sports uniform – would cost fifty dollars. For Mum, that was a fortnight's rent. She just didn't have that kind of money lying around. Because I was a scholarship kid in financial difficulty, the school gave us a rental agreement for the schoolbooks and the fancy calculator I would need for the maths and science classes, but in the end, Mum still had to ask Grandad for a handout.

I was so happy. I remember getting dressed in the pristine uniform of this unbelievably prestigious school and admiring myself in our grubby bathroom mirror. I was so proud. Not only would I get to go to this incredible school with all these amazing facilities, but that I'd earned that place myself.

Even better, I would be there with my best mate, Michael, who'd been born rich and had always been destined to attend TSS. I'd figured when high school came along we'd go our separate ways in life, but here we were.

Things were looking up. I couldn't wait for my first day at TSS. I remember hoping that if everyone at this school came from the same sort of family as Michael – wealthy, happy – then all my classmates would be just as cool and fun to hang around with as he was. I learned soon enough that Michael was the exception to the rule. More often than not, being born into exceptional wealth shaped you into a pretty ordinary person.

5

Where there's a will, there's a relative

I've seen firsthand the way money can fuck up a family; it happened all the time to the rich kids of TSS. In my work as the Coffin Confessor, I've seen even weirder intersections of money and family. The two are usually a pretty unhappy combination.

Mary lived in a gated retirement community on the Gold Coast. It was quite exclusive, a lovely retirement village in a prestigious, expensive neighbourhood. Her unit alone would have been worth a fair few million dollars.

So it wasn't as though Mary was living out her final days in poverty. She'd done quite well in life – her husband had worked for BHP for decades, then died in a workplace accident in the eighties. This was back when industry was heavily unionised, so the company made sure she was adequately compensated. The accident took her husband away, but the compensation gave her enough money to live comfortably for the rest of her life.

But in turn, she had passed that money on to her kids so they could set themselves up in life. She'd even remortgaged her own home to help them buy property. She'd done everything for her kids. And that was the problem.

Mary's story was a sad one. It seemed to me that she'd been a great mother, and an even better grandmother, and had raised a loving family. That had been her whole goal in life. She'd devoted every financial and emotional resource she had to making a better life for her kids, and she'd done it – it had all come true.

Everything was lovely, until she started dying, and then it all fell apart.

The moment it became clear she didn't have long left to live, her children started fighting over her money. Mary had been careful to make sure all the appropriate arrangements were in place to divide up her estate. She'd written her last will and testament, and already disclosed to the family how the assets would be divided and who would be inheriting what. But none of the children thought they'd been given enough, and even before Mary had passed away, they were contesting her will.

Apparently one of Mary's daughters was working with a lawyer to have changes made to the will, as one of the other daughters had gone off the rails and she felt that daughter wasn't deserving of anything. Naturally, this was causing a lot of bitterness between all the siblings. They were fighting viciously, literally standing over this poor woman's deathbed and dragging her into their squabbling.

It was really bad, her family acting despicably when she wasn't even in the ground yet. Everything she'd done in life, she'd done for her kids – and they didn't give a fuck. They wanted more.

Mary had tried to amend her will a couple of times to placate one child or another, but then one of them would find a lawyer to argue that, in her weakened state, she couldn't be relied upon to know her own mind.

Eventually, Mary grew so disgusted by the behaviour around her, she decided to have the last laugh. *You want to treat me this way? Fine. But I'm going to scorch the earth on my way out.*

So she called me from the hospital, where she'd been admitted and it had become clear that she would not be leaving while she drew breath. She asked me to go to her home, track down her will and destroy it. If her kids and their lawyers were going to put the screws on her, she was going to screw right out from under them.

With her will destroyed, the family would have to fight it out amongst themselves, rather than sniping at each other across her deathbed. By the time the dust settled, Mary would be long gone, and it wouldn't be her problem anymore.

I guess she hoped that if her children saw the desperate lengths they had driven her to, they would come to their senses, sit down and talk like adults. I didn't like her chances, but I wasn't about to refuse Mary's deathbed request.

Before I did anything, I looked into the legalities of what she was asking of me. I assumed there would be some kind of law in place to prevent me from physically destroying somebody's will, especially right before their death, but I was surprised to find there was none. Provided I had written permission from Mary to enter her home, and she had given me the means to do so, there was nothing to stop me.

To reach Mary's home in the gated community, I had to pass through a security gate, which she had given me the code to.

It wasn't hard to find her place – a modest little unit, comparatively, in amongst the very wealthy community. It occurred to me that she had really lived well below her means in an effort to give her kids every advantage.

Once inside, I looked in the bottom drawer of her dressing table, where she'd told me I'd find a tin containing a number of sealed envelopes, each addressed to a loved one. These I kept, in order to return them to Mary.

The largest envelope was marked 'My Will'. This one I burned. I set it on fire and let the ashes scatter on the wind, as per Mary's instructions. I filmed the whole thing so Mary could verify that her wishes had been carried out.

When I visited Mary for the final time, I showed her the video, pulling a chair close to her bed so she could see it clearly.

'Good. Thank you.' She smiled weakly, closed her eyes. 'I'm very grateful for everything you've done for me.'

I told her it was my pleasure. I was gathering up my things, getting ready to leave, when Mary reached out and rested her hand on my arm. Her skin was as soft and dry as crepe paper.

She motioned for me to stay. 'Before you go, could you do me one last favour?'

At her request, I set my phone number to private, to hide it from the person on the other end, and turned on the speaker so Mary could hear the conversation. I rang her eldest daughter, who had been the main belligerent in the fight over the will.

When she answered, I introduced myself and explained that I was a private investigator, hired by her mother. I told the daughter that, under Mary's instructions, I had destroyed her last will and testament.

There was a long pause, and then a blast of unbridled fury down the phone.

'How dare you!' the daughter screamed. 'Who the fuck do you think you are? I'm going to have you arrested, you dumb fucking piece of shit. Where are you? The cops are on their way. I'm going to fucking kill you.'

She went completely off her head. I remained impassive. I got death threats every other day of the week from one charming individual or another, so it was no skin off my nose. I wasn't worried about the police either – I'd double-checked with them before I carried out Mary's request.

So I just let the daughter vent. She didn't seem very happy with how her day was turning out.

All through the call, while her daughter had a meltdown, poor Mary gripped my arm. I could feel her shaking with silent laughter, but I'll never forget the look on her face as she listened to the daughter tear strips off me. She was holding a face washer against her face, trying not to make any noise because she had a very distinctive laugh, but there were tears running down her face. I can't imagine what she was feeling just then. A strange and sad situation.

After a minute of this, Mary patted me on the hand, indicating I could hang up.

'Have a lovely day,' I told the daughter, hanging up. I said my final goodbyes to Mary and went out into the sunshine.

How it all ended up, I'll never know, but I hope Mary's kids came to their senses in the end. She seemed like a lovely old lady, driven to desperation after dedicating her life to her kids. Maybe she did too much for them? In any case, from then on, if they wanted to fight over her money, they were going to have to fight amongst themselves. Job done.

* * *

I've got another client, a man who hasn't passed away yet, who is keeping a secret about money from his family. It's not what you think, whatever it is you're thinking. It's totally crazy, even by the standards of the job of crashing funerals.

This man approached me and indicated he wanted to hire me on the understanding that he wasn't dying, was actually in great health, but just wanted to make sure that a certain secret he'd been nursing for years would be revealed at his funeral.

This gentleman's secret is that he's never worked a day of his life. That's because very early in life he won the lotto, taking home an obscene amount of money. Millions and millions of dollars.

Right away he realised that if people knew how rich he was it would change everything. Everyone would treat him differently, and he would become a target for scams and hard-luck stories. He was just a decent bloke, he wanted a regular life, and so he didn't tell anyone, just invested the money and went on living.

It turned out he'd invested spectacularly well – he got even richer. That only made the problem worse.

He had to find some way to explain why he had so much money, so for years he's been pretending to go to work. Every morning he puts on a suit, gets in the car, and drives off to kill time for a day. He'll go and have a nice lunch, see a movie, whatever.

Everyone in his life thinks he's a genius businessman. It's gotten to the point where he can't possibly reveal his secret. I mean, after twenty years or however long of pretending to have a job, how do you turn around to your wife and explain that situation.

He knows it's a ridiculous conundrum, but he also thinks it's hilarious. Secretly, I think he actually really enjoys everyone thinking he's this brilliant business mind.

* * *

And then there was Martha. Martha was a real character. Funny as fuck, she took everything as it came and could see the funny side to anything. Even death.

Martha's attitude was very much that yes, she would be dead soon, and that was a bit of a problem, but it was a problem that everyone had sooner or later, so why worry about it?

A real old-fashioned eccentric, she was a hoarder. A hoarder of cash, specifically.

For some reason she didn't trust the banks. Instead, she had a compulsion to hide all her cash throughout her house. Lots of people in her generation have the habit of pocketing twenty bucks here and there, storing it in a safe place for a rainy day. Martha just took it a step further. Instead of one safe place – say, a biscuit tin – she'd stash money literally all over the house. In between couch cushions, in ceiling vents, in the Weet-Bix box.

When she paid me, she went and fetched an antique, plastic soap dish and pulled out all these old paper hundred-dollar notes from within it. That material for bank notes was phased out decades ago, but she'd kept the money in this slapdash hiding spot the whole time.

Martha's husband never caught on to her hoarding, although she kept trying to tell him. Throughout their life together she'd asked him to carefully check things before he got rid of them, because she might have stashed money in there. He'd throw out an expired can of soup he found at the back of a cupboard, and she'd freak out, because she'd washed out the tin and had hidden a hundred bucks inside.

She kept trying to get him to cop on to her habits, with little success. As the decades went on, her hoarding became more and more intense, and her husband got grumpier and grumpier. He kept right on throwing shit out when he thought he should.

And then, all of a sudden, Martha was dying. She was 100 per cent certain that although she'd begged her husband to go through everything in the house carefully, he simply wouldn't. The way she told it to me, he was liable to throw out a great deal of cash the next time he cleaned the house.

Martha was deadly serious about it, so she'd hidden a considerable amount of money in the pockets of all her coats, still hanging in her wardrobe. She hired me to go up to her husband at the wake, introduce myself, and read the following letter.

'Hi Donald, my love. Please make sure you go through my clothes before donating them. And don't forget that you're surrounded by the people that love us both – you only have to reach out, you grumpy old bastard. I love you, and thank you for everything you did for me. You made my life wonderful and filled it with love. Don, I'll be with you, so anytime you want to talk, I'll be listening. Love always, your baby. PS. I'm not joking, check the pockets of my clothes.'

It's very strange what matters to people at the end of their life. It's nice when they take the time to figure out it's not about the money. When you get to the end, you can't take it with you.

Although it sure is nice to have when you're starting out.

6

Charity case

My neighbourhood was so poor that on my first day of high school I managed to get beaten up before I even set foot on campus.

To get to TSS from the government housing estate I lived on, I had to ride to the other side of my suburb, and then another one over, putting me very much on the wrong side of the tracks. It was a long bike ride, and I had to climb up a big hill and then coast down the other side.

I was on my way, day one, really pumping the pedals to get up the hill, when a kid from my neighbourhood saw me. He took one look at me, puffing away in my fancy school uniform, and decided he didn't like it. As I passed, he threw this huge metal mop bucket at me, which cleaned me up and knocked me into the gutter.

Three other kids surrounded me, wanting to beat me up. While I needed to fight back, at the same time I didn't want to get my new uniform dirty. So I was weaving around, trying to dodge punches and hit back but still stay nice and pretty for TSS. Then I caught a hook to the face, and blood started pouring from my nose. That was an extra level of difficulty – fighting three guys while trying to hold my nose to stop the bleeding.

The fight lasted until I'd gotten a few good ones in and the other kids ran off. Once the coast was clear, I picked my bike up from where it had fallen and found the crash had buckled the front wheel. I stashed the bike in some nearby bushes, dusted myself off, and walked the rest of the way.

I thought I was doing fine, that I'd gotten away with it, until I got to the school and saw myself in a mirror. My shirt was soaked in blood, there were grass stains all over my pants, gravel stuck in my skin. All things considered, I was a mess.

I got bailed up by the first teacher who saw me.

'What happened to you?' he wanted to know.

'I . . . umm . . .' I didn't want to admit that I'd been fighting. 'I fell off my bike.'

'Best learn how to ride your bike then, shouldn't you, boy?'

From that day on, I knew never to wear my uniform while riding to school. Instead I'd wear normal clothes and pack my TSS uniform in my bag. I'd cycle past my neighbourhood's high school as quick as I could, then get changed into my uniform at school. That remained my routine for the next couple of years.

It wasn't a great start to my academic career at TSS, and it wasn't going to get much better from there.

* * *

The main hurdle for me was that I couldn't read or write. Although I knew the letters of the alphabet, I just couldn't make them behave themselves on their way from my eyes to my brain. Even when I tried to concentrate, they would swim around on the page.

I'd tried to teach myself the best I could, but the way I made sense of words was different to everyone else. I spelled the word 'cat' *K-A-T*, because I learned it from Kit-Kat wrappers. I was absolutely sure that's how it was spelled, and I could not understand why you would spell it with a fucking *C* – no more than my teachers could understand why I thought it made sense to use a *K*.

I could spell certain words as I heard them. The word 'look' made sense, and so did 'day'. But I couldn't comprehend the idea of a silent letter. For the fucking life of me I could not get my head around why someone would put a *K* in 'knife'. What the fuck was that about!

Nouns, pronouns, all that shit, I couldn't understand. I could read signs by spelling the letters out aloud, but the moment you abbreviated anything, it made no sense to me at all.

I know now that I'm dyslexic. If I'd had one teacher from the modern era who gave two shits, they would have caught it in a heartbeat. They would have been able to find an appropriate teaching method that allowed me to learn to read and write effectively. My life would have been completely different. Of course, that never happened.

From what I could see, no inspiring underdog stories were being written at TSS. No *Dead Poets Society*-style teachers with hearts of gold looking to improve the wellbeing and self-esteem of at-risk kids. Or if there were, I certainly never met them.

The teachers I had were either old boys who had essentially never left the school or ambitious teachers from outside the community who wanted to teach at one of the most prestigious schools in Queensland. In either case, they were terrible snobs. Posh men who thought themselves King Shit because they'd secured a job in the top ranks of teachers in the country.

They didn't know what to do with me. When each teacher discovered I couldn't read, they were outraged that they were expected to teach me. The attitude was, 'You've rewarded this kid who lives in a fucking trailer park with a position at our beloved school? And we've got to educate him? No way, we're not wasting our time.' They hated me from day one.

After a couple of weeks fumbling through the curriculum, a teacher sent me to a remedial class for kids who were struggling with basic arithmetic. Maths made sense to me, that was no problem, but the teacher there refused to have me.

'I'm not here to teach idiots,' he told me. 'Especially idiots who don't even pay for the privilege of coming to this school.'

'Alright,' I mumbled. 'See ya later.'

After that, teachers would just mark me as present and then send me off to do chores around the campus. There seemed to be this unspoken agreement amongst the whole faculty that, since they couldn't teach me, they would just treat me like hired help. Or worse.

'Oh, it's the Charity Case,' one teacher announced to the class on the first day of a new year. 'You sit in the back, Charity. Go sit on the floor and play with crayons.'

* * *

Naturally enough, the disrespect the teachers showed me was quickly adopted by the other boys at the school. I knew a few of them from primary, and I remember one day approaching Tim – a guy I'd been quite good mates with – while he was in a group playing handball. Despite my academic difficulties, I was still good at sports and loved to play when I got a chance, so I asked to join. I was sent away quickly enough, but not before the biggest bloke in the group yelled out to me.

'What are you even doing here, Charity?' he called. 'Your mum must be a prostitute. How else can you afford to come to this school?'

I remember the crunch and the pop of his nose breaking. That one punch put him on his arse, and he went straight to water. He sat there startled, holding his nose, and started crying. That shocked me more than any reprisal – where I was from, nobody went down from one punch, especially a big hulking bully like this guy.

I spun around to take on all his mates, who I assumed would be coming at me now, but they were all either backing away warily or bending down to console the bully.

Confused and disgusted, I remember looking at my former mates, including Tim, and spitting on the ground before walking away. I didn't get far. A prefect – one of the senior boys who kept an eye on the younger ones – grabbed me by the arm and ordered me to follow him to the headmaster's office. I refused, shrugging him off and storming away, only to be intercepted by a school official, who used his cane to whip me over the back of the legs and dragged me up to the headmaster's office.

While waiting outside the office, through the window I could already see a number of boys inside, answering questions about the incident. One of them was my old friend Tim, who I could see telling the headmaster all about the fight. From the way he was gesturing and pointing towards the hallway, I could tell he was blaming me for the fight.

When the headmaster finally called me into the office, he sat me down and frowned. I'd expected him to yell at me, and perhaps even to beat me with a cane, but instead he just sounded disappointed.

'You are from a different world to these boys, Robinson,' he said. 'You will have to learn – quickly – that they have options in life you never will. I've given you this chance so that, one day, you may be able to have what they have. Don't waste this opportunity. Use it. I don't want to find out that I made an error of judgment in choosing you.'

With that, I was sent back to class. I never spoke to Tim or those boys ever again.

* * *

In time, I realised that the headmaster was right. I quickly became aware that while there were regular levels of rich and poor, there were also extreme instances of each. In the same way that some people were dirt-poor – poorer than poor – there were also those who were filthy rich.

For the first year at TSS we were all the same age, looked more or less the same, and wore the same uniform, so I had no idea how wealthy some of my classmates were. But then they all started getting their driver's licences and coming to school in these unbelievable luxury cars, which their parents had bought for them. The school carpark was full of my classmates' BMWs and Jaguars. There was a sixteen-year-old kid driving a fucking Ferrari to rugby practice.

TSS was the sort of school that has a Latin motto, in this case 'Palmam qui meruit ferat'. That translates loosely as 'Let whoever earns the palm bear it'. This was somewhat ironic, given that the vast majority of boys attending the school were already so rich they would never need to earn anything.

It took two years of attending TSS before I stopped resenting the rich kids and started pitying them instead. I became aware that they lived in a world of greed and constant competition, not just between the students, but also between their parents. A certain level of extreme wealth brings with it such severe status anxiety that it might be nearly as miserable as having nothing.

The desire to have more and more money – and show it off – brought the parents of many of my classmates to financial ruin. Watching these parents self-destruct, and the consequent collapse of their family units, showed me that the gap between me and them was not as big as I had thought. In some ways, they fell into greater poverty than mine, because I was already there and living it, and had been all my life.

My circumstances gave me a burning drive to find a way out; I knew physical hardship could be overcome. Theirs was a more profound poverty – a poverty of the mind, of the soul. Perhaps, in this one way, I was more fortunate than them. Insatiable greed is a kind of starving of the spirit. I knew what it was like to be hungry, but these kids were growing up with a craving for 'more' that could never be satisfied.

Before I was ostracised at school, I'd had a chance to visit friends' houses – homes that looked like five-star hotels. Marble floors, gold and brass trimmings. Ten bedrooms for a four-person family. Bathrooms with floor-to-ceiling windows offering some of the most mind-blowing views imaginable. Games rooms filled with pool tables, pinball machines. Swimming pools, tennis courts.

These homes were reached by private roads and through security gates, or across a river with a chauffeured boat. I met butlers, nannies and au pairs who were so well-dressed and well-spoken that I found it hard to differentiate between my mates' families and their hired help. Especially those times I walked into a room and caught the father of the house slapping the nanny on the arse, or getting it on with the au pair in the spa. The headmaster was right: it was a different world to the one I was from.

So I shut up. I avoided fights, played soccer and hung out on my own.

At the end of the year the other kids were handed report cards, which brought them either joy or anxiety when they took them home to their families. My teachers never gave me a report, and my mother never asked about them. But, year after year, I was advanced to the next grade by teachers who just couldn't be bothered having me in their class again the following year.

It was an unhappy situation all around. The students hated me, the teachers hated me, I hated it there, and my mum hated the fact that I was going there. The idea that I was now a private-school kid pissed my mum off something shocking. It didn't matter that I was there on a scholarship in recognition of talent – when you lived in commission housing, when your only income came from benefits and the pokies, and you couldn't make rent, you weren't supposed to have a kid going to a school that cost $50,000 a year in fees.

Because of that, she got a lot of shit from our neighbours. They thought it wasn't right, that I had got above my station. Once upon a time Mum could have hit up a neighbour and borrowed a little money for a loaf of bread and some milk, but now they would just laugh in her face. If you had a kid at one of the most expensive schools in the country, you shouldn't have to beg.

It added an extra layer of humiliation to her life, and she resented me for it.

And through this all, I never knew when Grandad would pop over, find a way to get me alone and have his way with me. So I began to avoid coming home. I'd sleep in the park, or in the toilets down by the river, and get up before dawn to sneak back into the school and use the showers there to clean up before class.

* * *

A few years earlier, Michael might have been around to help me through all this, but it wasn't to be at TSS. From day one, we'd been separated. He'd been placed in classes for high achievers, while I'd been put out to pasture in classes for remedial learning. Even though we technically went to the same school, we may as well have been on different planets.

Naturally, we drifted apart. He grew to inhabit the place in society his privilege afforded him, while I grew more isolated with each passing school day. It got to the point where the only time we'd spend together was at soccer training, when we'd go on these long-distance runs to build up our stamina. We'd talk a little then, but mainly I was just trying to keep pace with him.

Then, in the summer holidays between years 9 and 10, I lost Michael completely. The last time I spoke to him, I ran into him at school, and he told me he was going on a ski trip for the holidays.

'Where are you going?' I said. 'I'd love to come.'

'Switzerland,' he said. 'I dunno, I think it's just family.'

'Switzerland! Fuck, that'd be cool! I've never seen snow.'

We shook hands and I told him I'd talk to him when he got back. But he never came back. Word reached me that he'd gone out skiing after a particularly nasty blizzard, and while the course had been cleared by the authorities, nobody had realised that a large sign warning of a steep cliff had blown down in the storm. Michael went straight over the edge of the cliff, and he never came back up.

I was devastated, but it was nothing compared to what his parents went through. They were absolutely shattered, just unable to continue with their lives on the Gold Coast. They packed everything up, sold their house and moved away. That was painful too, watching them suffer like that. They were more like a family to me than anyone back at home.

Sometime after Michael died, I went for a run – cross country, long distance, my first since he'd passed away. I'd never had someone I cared about die before, and I didn't know how to feel. I found myself talking to Michael, just chatting to him as I ran along. Telling him about school, how I wished I could have seen the snow with him, how much I missed him.

It was strange, I guess, like I suddenly had an imaginary friend. Anyone else would say he wasn't real, but he was real to me, and he's been with me ever since.

All through the rest of school, now and again, Michael would pop into my head and we'd have a chat. I guess his ghost was the closest thing I had to feeling safe. For the time that I knew him, he was the best mate I ever had, and I never imagined that I'd be alive when he wasn't. He had such a good life, and it seemed so unfair that he would be the one to lose it. So I kept him alive, in my own way, and I've been talking to him ever since.

7

Deathstiny

There are some losses people can't get over. The things people ask me to do for them from their deathbed are always painfully honest; for some, it may be the most honest they've been with themselves their whole lives.

A last request – the thing someone can't let go of when they're out of time – is as unique as a fingerprint. Sometimes people seem genuinely surprised by what is most important to them, once it comes down to the wire. I know they surprise me.

Generally I try to fulfil any request. I figure if it's a client's last wish in the world, it's gotta be important to them. So if it's not illegal, and it's not going to hurt anyone, I'll do what I can. I do my due diligence, some basic PI work to determine if they're telling the truth, but they always are. Nobody is going to lie while on their deathbed. You'd have to be pretty fucked in the head.

Which is not to say that some of the requests aren't pretty fucked in the head.

One guy wanted me to kill his dog. He loved this dog more than anything; it was the only thing he cared about in the world – he had nothing else in his life. He couldn't stand the thought of being without his dog, and since he was going to die before the poor mutt, he wanted to take it with him. A pharaoh's funeral sort of a thing – they'd go into the afterlife together.

That was a request I denied.

'I can't do that, mate,' I told him. 'If you want, I'll find the dog a new home, but I'm not going to murder him.'

The guy agreed, and I went out and rehomed the dog. The poor thing was fifteen years old! It ended up dying a couple of weeks after its owner anyway. I guess that was a happy ending.

Another client, a young woman, Suze, asked me to confront her brother after her death. Basically she wanted me to deliver a message that let him know she hated him and that he had ruined her life. She was a drug addict, which had begun with her self-medicating to deal with the abuse he'd subjected her to.

In the end I declined her request too. I didn't want to put myself in a position where I was confronting someone who'd abused a child. If it turned physical, I could see myself ripping his head off and getting myself into a whole world of trouble with the law. There was a good chance that if I had to hit him, I wouldn't stop until he was dead. I wasn't about to put my family through the ordeal of me going to prison, so I declined.

Suze told me that the reason hers was a deathbed request was that she was planning on taking her own life. I did my best to talk to her about it. I was honest with her; I told her that I didn't know what she was going through, but that I'd had my own experience of being suicidal.

All I could ask her to do was consider two important questions. One, as long as she was still alive, it was probably for a reason – an important one. What was that reason? Two, if she were to die, who else would it affect? Who would miss her? Was there someone in her life who would be more hurt by her death than what the end of suffering would mean for her?

That's what had worked for me. But at the end of the day, all I could do was try to guide her to get help. I could intervene, call the cops, a psych ward, but ultimately it was in her hands.

People deal with trauma in their own way. It's personal. The damage from abuse, from loss – we all find a way to keep going. Or we don't.

There have been times when I've been very close to taking my own life, when I've been overcome by this profound sense of peace at the realisation that I could end all my hurt and regret.

I've always found a way back from that brink, though. I found ways to cope, and things that mattered so much to me that they were worth living for. There's a million reasons why someone might want to die, but finding a reason to keep living after being broken? That's something special.

For some people it's love. For others it's hate. For others still it's revenge. I can empathise with all three.

8

Can't break me

I was fifteen years old, and I was living on and off the streets. My time living rough had taught me to fight, had taught me that I was capable of looking after myself and surviving almost anything. There wasn't a day I didn't think about Grandad, though. Throughout the day, memories of what he'd done to me would pop into my head unbidden. Those thoughts left me panicked and breathless. At night, I'd wake up gasping from nightmares where he was having his way with me.

Grandad used to brew his own beer in the shed behind the house, which was big enough for his brewing equipment as well as garden tools and our lawn mower. Brewing his own beer was far cheaper than buying it in the bottle shop, and according to him his beer was stronger and tasted better. But it was also more dangerous – now and again the bottles would explode under the pressure of fermentation. When they popped, you could hear it from inside the house.

The bottles were neatly arranged on the shelves by the date they were bottled, so Grandad knew which ones he should drink first. Everything was kept neatly in its own space, so there was enough room for him to take me in and molest me when he felt like it.

I'll never forget the first time. I was kicking the soccer ball around the backyard; Nanna was taking a nap before dinner, as she wasn't feeling too well after a few afternoon drinks with Grandad. Knowing Grandad couldn't hurt me as long as Nanna was around, I'd felt safe before she'd gone to sleep.

I heard Grandad calling me from the shed, and when I got there he met me out the front, telling me to take off my boots before entering the shed. I'd never been allowed inside before; I could hardly believe the amount of beer it held.

As I examined the bottles, Grandad stood behind me and put his hands on my shoulders. He asked me if I had touched myself lately.

I began to shake, partly out of shock, because I knew that Nanna was asleep just metres away. All I had to do was scream out for her. But I couldn't make myself do it. I was frozen, paralysed, unable to react at all.

When I was only nine, I'd learned to make myself vanish whenever Grandad touched me. I'd made a safe place for myself in my mind, a place entirely of my imagination that only I could visit. This 'safe place' is where I would go whenever I was being abused, but also when I was feeling sad or lonely. I would leave my body far behind, sometimes spending hours there, just staring into space with my mouth wide open like I was catching flies – my mother's words.

Grandad started to undress me, lifting my shirt over my head. He took off my shorts and underwear, leaving me completely naked except for a pair of socks. From where I stood, I could see out through the shed door, but there was no sign of Nanna or my mum, or anyone else for that matter. So I closed my eyes and went to my safe place, waiting for Grandad to finish what he was doing. Unfortunately, when I did that, I lost control of my bladder and wet myself.

I had no control over it, I didn't even realise what had happened until Grandad brought me back into the room with a frustrated smack on the back of my legs. The blow knocked me forward into a shelf of beer, which toppled over and exploded with the force of a small bomb.

'You dumb, stupid, little fucking idiot,' he hissed.

Grandad quickly picked up my clothes and told me to get dressed. Once I had my clothes back on, he dragged me to the door through the smashed beer bottles. I stepped on a piece of glass, cutting my foot. Noticing the blood, I sat down outside the shed to take off my sock. But Grandad approached and ripped the sock off my foot. In a voice loud enough for anyone watching to hear, he said that it was only a small cut and that I shouldn't have been playing with a soccer ball in his shed anyway.

Later that afternoon, Nanna woke up feeling much better. As she made dinner, Grandad told her that I had kicked my soccer ball into the shed, ruining some of his home-brew.

Nanna was very annoyed. 'Silly boy. You should know better than to be playing soccer near Grandad's shed.'

It seemed that Grandad always had an excuse for my cuts and bruises, and why I had transformed from a cheerful, confident boy into a scared, traumatised one. He would look straight at me while telling lies to cover up what he had been doing. Both my mum and Nanna believed every word. And so it would continue.

* * *

In my teenage nightmares, and in my memory, Grandad was the man he'd seemed to me as a child. A giant – strong and dominant. The backbone of the family and the man of the house. When he said something was to be done, it was done without question. If you crossed him, he was someone to be feared. Even at fifteen, it was impossible for me to think about him any other way.

At the same time, I couldn't let go of thoughts of revenge. I stayed awake through long nights on the street, brooding on how I could make him pay for what he had done to me.

I was convinced that confronting him would take away all of the hurt I was carrying. I thought that the emotional burden would be lifted, giving me freedom from the past.

One afternoon, I finally found the courage to do it. I turned up at Grandad's house, ready to confront him, only to find he and Nanna were out.

It had taken me weeks to psych myself up, and I didn't know what to do with the adrenaline pumping through my system. I decided to break in and steal what I could – cash, jewellery, appliances I could sell for money to buy food.

Once I'd done it, the act of housebreaking seemed so simple, I then decided to call on my uncle and aunt's home and do the same.

Looking back, this was the behaviour of a boy who was desperately crying out for help. But I was out of control, and refused to believe that I needed help. So did a family member, who worked out that it was me who had broken into both homes. He and a couple other men decided to teach me a different kind of lesson.

They found the unit I was squatting in, kicked down the door and beat me savagely.

Between punches and kicks they demanded to know how I could steal from my own family. 'How could you do this to your grandparents? What did they ever do to you?'

When they were finished, they stood above my battered and broken body.

'Sort your shit out,' one of them spat. 'There's more where this came from if you don't.'

* * *

It was months until I again found the courage to confront Grandad. I had learned that my nanna was overseas on a holiday and he was home alone. It was now or never.

I was staying in Surfers Paradise by then, and I rode my bike from there all the way to Grandad's house, which gave me about forty minutes to think about what I was going to do and how I was going to do it.

But when I arrived, I rode my bike up and down the street probably twenty times or more, still gathering my rage. It was a bright night with a full moon and a sky full of stars, around 7 p.m., and all up and down the street you could see people preparing dinner or watching television in their lounge. Through the sliding front door of Grandad's house, I could see him sitting in front of his TV, sucking on his home-brew.

Finally, I forced myself to stop and park my bike.

As I walked up to the house, I passed the big blue Ford Fairlane my grandad had used to drive me to quiet places and abuse me. That made me lose it. My body began shaking, my throat dried up and sweat ran down my face. I could hear my heart beating as though it were outside my chest – it sounded like the whole neighbourhood should be able to hear it.

Panting, I stopped and tried to compose myself. But the more I tried that, the faster my heart beat. My shirt was soaked with sweat.

I turned and walked away, back towards my bike. With each step I felt calmer. But when I reached my bike, I could not bring myself to leave.

'Come on,' I told myself, breathing deep. 'Fuck you, you gutless fuck. Are you just going to ride away like a scared little fuck? Get the fuck back there and do this.'

I turned back, once more, determined. I could see images of me being abused – in the car, in the shed, in this house, the bathroom, the bedroom, the lounge room. Each memory made me angrier, and with that anger came strength.

Suddenly, I was there, at the door. Through the gauzy white curtain I could see my grandad. I knocked three times, loudly and assertively. I saw him startle and head towards the door. When he recognised me, he unlocked the door with a rather confused and angry look on his face.

The moment the door slid open, I reached through and grabbed him by the throat with my right hand.

Walking him back into the living room, I increased my grip, feeling my fingers tighten on his windpipe. He clutched at my hand, struggling to breathe. Tears flowed down his face and he tried to say something, but between his gasping and my pulse hammering in my ears I couldn't make out what.

Then I saw myself. I realised that I held my grandfather's life in my hands. I had to make a choice.

I could take his life from him easily, but then what would that make me? Cross that line once and you never go back.

It had never occurred to me before, not for a second of my life, that I was capable of stopping him or hurting him. Now I saw him as he was: a weak, sick, twisted old man.

If I'd known that as a small child, he could never have hurt me. And now he could never hurt me again.

I released my grip, and he fell to the floor gasping, rubbing his throat.

He tried to say he was sorry, but I wasn't interested in hearing that word from him. All I wanted was to see him cower, for him to know how it felt to be scared and helpless. I wanted him to know that I hated him, that I had spared his life only because he wasn't worth it. I didn't need to say or do anything more than that.

As I left, I passed the shed where he made his home-brew, and where he had beaten and abused me. I swung the door open, and sure enough, there was his brewery and his precious beer, still neatly arranged in rows. On the spur of the moment, I decided to smash every bottle and destroy the brewery, hoping that this would somehow make me feel better. It didn't – it wasn't the shed or the beer I needed to destroy, it was all those memories of abuse I had been holding on to.

* * *

As I rode away, I was overcome. I felt strong, assertive and tough, but also ashamed. Part of me was disgusted by what I had done. And all of me felt terribly sad that this is what my childhood had amounted to – destroying the home-brew setup of a paedophile and abuser, and the only father figure I'd ever known.

Confused by what I felt, I started to make my way back to the familiar streets of Surfers Paradise. I stopped in a park by the Broadwater, to sit and contemplate what had happened. I let my bike crash on the pavement, then sat, staring blankly out at the night. The moon was shimmering on the water, which danced with the help of a light breeze. Boats were moored at different locations along the river, with lights visible on most.

A popular spot for families, the park was filled with swings and picnic tables, but it was too late for all that. It was just me, alone. I realised that I'd been alone my entire life. Now that I knew for certain that I had nothing and no one, the only thing I wanted was my mum.

I let out a scream that echoed across the water, then started crying uncontrollably. There was nothing I could do to bring myself under control. I had truly believed that confronting Grandad would bring me peace. Instead, I felt worse than I ever had.

Thoughts of what had happened to me, what I had done and what would happen next crowded for space in my mind and body. The thought occurred to me, not for the first time, that ending my life might be the best option.

I wept for what seemed like hours, wept until I simply had no more tears.

Finally, I felt it was time to move on. I turned to collect my bike, only to find it gone. While I had been sobbing inconsolably, someone had come by and stolen it. I let out a sound that was neither a laugh nor a sob, and turned to the sky. 'Good one!' I yelled at God. I hoped he, at least, could see the humour in the situation.

I left on foot, heading towards the bright lights of Surfers Paradise. That was my home now, and I knew exactly where to go for food and shelter.

As I made my way, vehicles whizzed by, and as each bus or truck rumbled past I contemplated jumping in front of it.

But then a car parked on the side of the road caught my attention. The interior light had been left on and, peering inside, I saw the keys were still in the ignition.

I looked around to see if anyone was watching. Once I was sure the coast was clear, I opened the driver's side door, turned the key, put the car into gear, and drove off, keeping one eye on the mirror to make sure nobody was coming after me.

Once I'd calmed down a little, I rolled down the window and cruised towards Surfers. I was just getting close to the bridge to Surfers when I realised that the cars in front were slowing down. It turned out the police had set up a breath-testing site – right before the bridge, where cars had no way of turning off to avoid them.

As I slowed down, a huge police officer with a mean face directed me to drive up to him for testing. For a moment, I panicked. I considered flooring the accelerator and steering into the cop to run him over, then driving off as fast as I could. But something inside me shifted. After everything I'd been through that night, what was one thing more?

Suddenly I was totally calm. I wound down my window and greeted the cop in a loud, mature voice.

'Had anything to drink tonight?' he said, bored and surly.

'Not a drop.'

He asked me to blow into the breathalyser, which back then looked like a plastic lunch bag with a straw that changed colour. The officer clocked my test as it came back negative, then leaned into the window and scanned the inside of the car.

'Okay, on your way,' he grunted. 'But I wouldn't leave my wallet on the back seat like that if I were you. Lotta thieves around.'

I nodded calmly, put the car in first, and cruised off towards the bright lights of the city. Once I was over the bridge, I turned down a side street and parked. I reached into the back seat and, sure enough, there was a brown wallet.

Inside it was more money than I had ever seen in my life – $800, all in large fifty-dollar notes. I also found a plastic card with the word 'Metway' printed on it. I'd never had a bank account, but I knew that adults used these to get money out of bank machines after opening hours. A search of the wallet turned up some business cards and a note with a four-digit number written on the back of it. I figured this was the code that would grant me access to the money in the account. Again I turned my face to the heavens, but this time I laughed and said a polite, 'Thank you.'

I found a Metway ATM and tried the card, punched in the PIN. There was a pause, a whirr, and then small green words appeared on the screen asking me how much money I wanted to withdraw.

'Hell yes,' I said.

I tried different combinations until I had emptied the account of a total of $1300.

I placed the card back in the wallet, then walked into the closest all-night coffee shop. There I handed the wallet to a waitress, telling her I found it on the seat I was about to sit on.

'Thanks, love,' she said. 'Appreciate your honesty. Now, what'll you have?'

I ordered the most luxurious meal I could imagine: a banana, cheese and bacon toasted finger, and a large hot chocolate.

I was just a kid, after all. Barely fifteen. I still had so much to learn. But that night I learned for sure that revenge wouldn't ever bring me peace. And that God has a sense of humour after all.

* * *

The only other time I saw my grandad after that night was when he was on his deathbed, surrounded by some family members who were quite upset. I played my part and made myself cry as they ushered me into his room. I sat on the bed next to him and rested my hand on his forehead, whispering in his ear, 'Rot in hell, you fucker.' I turned to the doorway and told the family standing there that I'd whispered, 'I forgive you.'

At Grandad's funeral I waited behind until everyone had left. A young guy started to shovel dirt into the grave. He looked at me with a grin and said, 'Do you want to do this, mate? Some people get satisfaction out of it.'

'Fuck yes,' I said without hesitation – how could I not? He handed me the shovel and I filled that fucking hole with as much dirt as I could manage.

The young guy said, 'Mate, either you loved that person or hated their guts – either way, I'm glad you're here. It's nearly full.' I spat on the grave. 'Yep, hated him, hey. Take care, bro.'

And with that, I turned and walked away.

9

Home sweep home

It's not that I have a problem with authority. I wouldn't even say that I'm suspicious of it. It's more a matter of encountering, nearly every day of my life, authority that has been granted to the wrong people. Preachers, teachers, parents, police – anyone who claims authority is someone who believes that, for whatever reason, they have the right to tell someone else how to live. Generally, I've found it's rare they do this for good reasons.

For much of human history, society has been run by people who are in charge because they've told enough people they should be in charge. After that, they build systems to make their power seem legitimate.

Look at politics – it doesn't matter what you believe in, chances are that the person who represents you politically is a fucking sociopath. In fact, look at pretty much any institution that wields power over ordinary people. Nine times out of ten, you're going to find that the sweet, kind and generous are taken advantage of. They say the meek shall inherit the earth, and that may be true, but it's often in a pretty sorry state by the time it gets to them.

In late 2018, a woman named Pam engaged me to help put her house in order. Poor Pam was a really sweet older lady – courteous, kind-hearted, sweet-natured – who'd just been absolutely fucked over by the world. She was sick with motor neurone disease, which was swiftly robbing her of mobility and speech. Her condition was deteriorating rapidly, which was terrible for her, and complicated further by the fact that her son had a disability and relied on her.

Until recently, Pam had been living on a farm in rural New South Wales, part of an evangelical Christian community. When she'd become too ill to keep living on the property, she'd had to leave behind her pet birds and other items of concern.

When Pam called me, her sister was making arrangements to visit the farm and help pack it up. But that would have seen her finding some personal items in the bedroom that Pam did not want her very conservative Christian sister finding – things of a sexual nature.

'Yep, no problem,' I said. 'On my way.'

From the embarrassed way that Pam spoke about her belongings, I was expecting something really salacious. The sort of filthy pornography that no one wants their next of kin stumbling upon when packing up the silverware and the good china. But when I got there, and found what she'd had in mind, it was nothing out of the ordinary: some lingerie, a few racy books. Nothing anyone should feel ashamed about. It made me wonder what had been said to her to make her so afraid of judgment.

While I was searching the place, I got a call from the sister, who'd learned I was making a sweep of the home.

'Hello?' I said, picking up the phone, but she was already jumping down my throat.

'Don't you go to Pam's house now. Don't you fuckin' dare! I'll be there in a day or two.'

'Too late,' I said, innocently enough. 'I'm already here.'

She didn't care for that, and she chewed my ear off until I put down the phone. I've gotta say, Pam was one of the sweetest, most thoughtful women you could ever hope to meet. Her sister . . . not so much.

I went on packing up Pam's things and, as I did, I started to become quite emotional. I really liked Pam, she was great to talk to – just bursting with life and kindness, even as weak as she was. And now that I was in her home, where she'd spent her whole life, pretty much, it struck me that she'd had a really hard life.

Pam was properly religious. She and her husband had settled in this evangelical community, which was really quite isolated. The properties here had lots of land, but few people. Her husband had been the administrator of the local church, and a real upstanding member of the community – in public. To be honest, it seems like he was a real shitty bloke.

Pam's son was born in 1964, and during his childhood he was diagnosed with a disease related to polio. This shouldn't have happened in the first place – the polio vaccine had been around for ages, and the last epidemic in Australia happened a decade before the boy was born, but Pam's husband had refused to have the boy vaccinated. Still, it shouldn't have been too big a deal, except he also refused to allow Pam to get any treatment for their son.

The way he saw it, if his son was ill, that was just a test of the family's faith. The boy might die, sure, but if he did, that was God's will. In his evangelical faith, it would have been acting against God to save his son's life.

The boy did live, but the polio took his legs. The rest of his body recovered fine, and his mind was unaffected, but he would never walk again.

I get the impression the husband fucked off not long after that, leaving Pam pretty much to fend for herself. His cowardice meant that Pam had had to care for her son all alone on this isolated property with nothing but farms in every direction. The neighbours were nice, but they were still some distance away, and she had a property to maintain as well as looking after her son. No, not an easy life at all.

The first step of the job she'd hired me to do was to retrieve her birds, who were alive and well. I ended up rehoming them with her son. He'd already had to move away to another property that better suited his needs when his mum's mobility started to go. He was a lovely bloke – smart and kind, but sad. It broke my fucking heart, to think what a different life this guy might have had if he didn't have this God-bothering tyrant for a dad.

I guess that's something that speaks to me. Imagine being someone that denies their son treatment for a deadly illness. How could you look at yourself in the mirror every day? Your son suffering like that because you were too proud to question your faith for half a second. What sort of person does that?

Then half a century later, I happen to come along and hear their stories, right at the end of someone's life. And all I can do is sit there, and listen, and think how hard it must have been.

Why didn't somebody help them? Why didn't someone just fucking go in there and break down the door and rip them out of there?

Because that just doesn't happen. It didn't happen back then, and it doesn't happen today. Every day you hear stories of women living in fear. Men too, of course, but so many women have suffered so much at the hands of blokes who abuse their family.

Stories like Pam's do get to me. They hold a little place in my heart. I guess I feel for anyone who's been subjected to abuse. I know what it's like to be that kid, waking up in terror every morning because the day ahead is going to be worse than a fucking nightmare. That's how it was for me, and nobody ever came and kicked my door down to rescue me. Nobody ever came to help. Life doesn't work that way.

10

Never smile at a paedophile

The money in that wallet meant that I never had to go back to my mum's house. I was able to survive on my own for ages. I never went home – I stayed on the streets. I slept in parks or down by the beach for days at a time, then weeks.

When I could, I would loiter at school, especially when all the dormitory boys who could afford to were off on camp. During that time I got to meet the boys who had been held back from going on camp, as punishment for smoking or academic underachievement. From them I learned everything there was to know about the school – the inner room of the clock tower, hidden doors and storerooms in the old buildings. It became very exciting, working out how to escape or hide from a teacher, or knowing how to cross secretly from one side of the campus to the other without anyone spotting you.

I learned the routines and rhythms of the school: the exact times that teachers were in meetings, where and when they met and who they were meeting with. I watched delivery drivers and couriers, working out when the laundry service would collect the dormitory students' washing. I worked out that I could duck in and steal a nice clean shirt, swap it out for my own, have it taken away, laundered by the school and returned to the rich kid's room, then do it all over again.

There were limitless opportunities for an entrepreneurially minded kid. The student body had immense financial resources, and they were prepared to pay well for their little extra privileges.

To begin with, I learned that some seniors would sneak out at night to party. They would arrange their bed sheets to make it look as if they were sleeping, then catch a taxi into the party-district lights of Surfers Paradise. There they would smoke, do drugs, drink, party with girls, then return like nothing had ever happened.

I counted beds in dorms, figured out which kids were regularly going out partying and on which nights, and realised there were spare beds for the taking. I could just wait for the boys to leave, jump into a bed for a good night's sleep, then sneak out again before sunrise when the housemaster would begin his rounds and wake the boys for breakfast.

One morning, the senior whose bed I'd borrowed returned early. I was shaken awake by a drunk, stoned older kid who wanted to know what I was doing in his bed.

'I saw you sneak out and thought you would get in trouble. I wanted to make sure there'd be someone in the bed if the house-master checked,' I said.

I watched the confused kid digest this bit of information, and realised that this was an opportunity staring me blearily in the face.

'I'll do it again,' I said, thinking quick. 'For a price.'

For the next eighteen months, as word about my services got around, I became a full-time boarder at the school.

I ate breakfast and dinner in the dining hall, then retired to a dorm or waited for one of the seniors of the school to let me know which bed was available.

Some of the seniors paid good money to have me sleep in their bed, as insurance against a spot check by teachers patrolling the dorms. A teacher would knock on the door, and I'd wave a hand and yell out that I was trying to sleep. Then I would slip out, slink to the next dorm, and do the same thing for another student.

Eventually, I extended my services to include helping the boys sneak out and get to Surfers Paradise undetected. I'd go down to the boat shed and borrow a little motorised tinnie, then collect a boatload of senior boys and taxi them over to the party district. I'd charge each student two bucks for the privilege, and before long I was making a decent living.

My income increased further when, after a few months, word got around that I knew my way around the Gold Coast. I became known as a kid who could find things.

With all my old friends from the wrong side of the tracks, I had connections to the street and could easily procure an abundance of alcohol or other recreational substances. The money was so good, in fact, that it supported me all through the rest of my time at TSS, keeping me clothed, fed, dressed, and even leaving me with a little pocket money to go to the movies, which I'd never done before.

It was at this time in my life that I first learned how to see opportunities and exploit them. I could buy a foil of marijuana for $20 on the street, for example, and sell it to the clueless rich kids in the years above me for $100. I didn't consider it ripping them off – it was just simple commerce. They got to party, and I got them their substances without any risk to them or their reputations. This is how rich kids have operated since the dawn of time.

I had understood from day one that I was out of my depth, that I could never compete with those boys on a social level, but it wasn't until the headmaster told me off for fighting – only the second time we'd ever spoken – that I realised just how different their lives were.

For these boys, TSS wasn't just an opportunity, it was an obligation. Their enrolment in such an elite school was just another status symbol to be displayed by their parents, no different from the shining cars in the driveway and the glamorous international holidays. The pressure that came with that was terrible in its own way. There was never any opportunity to make mistakes, or to feel really free from the shadow of parental expectations.

In addition to all that, the school had its own secrets. Terrible, horrific fucking secrets. I was going to find out about those soon enough.

* * *

It took some months after choking and pushing my grandad to the ground before I found the courage to finally speak to someone about what he'd done to me for all those years. The pressure of keeping the secret was becoming impossible for me to handle. I had to confide in someone.

I decided to tell Mr X, one of my teachers at school. I had a better rapport with him than most of the other teachers. He was kind to me, and took time to explain things when the others refused to condescend to teaching a charity case like me.

There was a school chaplain who we were supposed to be able to turn to for support, and this one was actually quite nice to me, but I just didn't trust priests. Years earlier I'd tried to turn to a priest who I'd met through a friend for help. But he'd shut me down, told me that I should be ashamed of what I was telling him. He instructed me to try and forget what had happened, and not to make trouble. As a consequence, in my eyes all clergy were in it together. Going to a priest for help would just be running from the arms of one paedophile into the arms of another.

So Mr X would be my confidant.

One morning, after I had left the dormitory I was crashing in, while the other boys were at breakfast, I approached Mr X and asked if I could talk to him about something personal, saying that I needed help with a serious matter. He looked very concerned, and he kindly suggested that I drop by his office after school that day.

All day I wrestled with myself over whether to turn up. The thought of telling someone what had been done to me made me physically ill, but the thought of holding on to it forever seemed just as bad.

In the end, I decided against it. I was undoing my bike lock with shaking hands, to escape to the streets, when another student ran up to me with a message that Mr X was wondering where I was.

He was a boy I was friendly with, but a bit of a teacher's pet, and a stubborn bastard. I knew it would be no use arguing with him. We set off to Mr X's office.

Weirdly, for years afterwards I blamed that boy for what happened next, although looking back, he couldn't have known.

Inside the office, Mr X sat me down and tried to calm me down. Eventually, I was comfortable enough to speak, slowly at first, but then the whole story came gushing out of me.

He listened, his face drawn, and thanked me for confiding in him.

'It must be such a relief for you to finally talk to someone,' he said. Now he understood why my grades had been so poor, my homework neglected, my sports and study-group participation so erratic.

He told me that his door was always open, but that he could not promise to keep this confidential, although he would do so for the foreseeable future.

* * *

As the weeks passed, I began to feel better. The thick knot of anxiety that had been tied in my chest for years began to loosen. I felt physically stronger; I was faster and more confident on the soccer field, and my coach began to be impressed for the first time since the beginning of my scholarship. My grades started to improve, as did almost every other aspect of my school life. I began to regret not putting my faith in Mr X earlier.

That was until one random Friday afternoon, when he summoned me. I'd just climbed out of the pool when a prefect approached and told me that Mr X had asked me to come to his office so we could talk. I had barely had enough time to dry myself and put on my sports shirt, so my swimmers were still wet when I knocked on his door.

'Come in,' he said. 'Shut the door behind you.'

Mr X motioned me to come and stand before his chair. He asked how I had been and if I needed anything from him. I told him I was fine, actually doing much better than I had been.

He smiled. 'Good,' he said. 'I'm glad.'

Then he placed his hands on my hips, looked me in the eyes, and said, 'I'll always be there for you.'

I was a little uncomfortable, but felt assured that he genuinely wanted to help me.

Then he tightened his grip and pulled me closer to him.

'You're shaking,' he said. 'Are you cold, or just nervous?'

Truthfully, I was both. But before I could say anything, he placed his palm over the front of my wet swimmers.

'Is this where your grandfather touched you?' he asked me. He reached into his own pants and began playing with himself. 'Is this what he did?'

My legs turned to jelly. All the confidence and strength I'd built up in recent weeks deserted me. I felt winded, as though I was being suffocated. The tears I thought had all but dried up returned and rolled silently down my cheeks. The windowless office suddenly seemed no larger than the corner store's back room where my grandfather had first abused me, all those years ago. Nobody would come in here unless I screamed, and that seemed imposs-ible. I was trapped, helpless with shock. I couldn't make a sound.

Once Mr X was done, he sighed and stood up abruptly.

'You're going to have to start trying harder around here,' he said in a stern voice. 'Your grades need to improve dramatically.'

With that he opened his office door and walked out, leaving me to follow meekly.

I went straight to my locker and got changed into dry clothes. I was crying so hard that another boy approached and asked if I was okay.

'I'm fine,' I snapped, wiping at my tears. 'I'm fine.'

I rode away, and cried all afternoon. I was upset and confused by what Mr X had done to me, but most of all I was disgusted and angry with myself for letting it happen.

Whenever I saw my reflection in a mirror or window, I hated what I saw. That weak, pathetic face staring back at me – I'd spit at it.

When I was alone, I would scream at my reflection, as though my anger could somehow transform me like the Incredible Hulk, giving me the inner strength I needed to defend myself.

* * *

Mr X continued to abuse me whenever he got the chance. I never knew when I would be summoned to his office – the knock at the door of the classroom, then a polite, bored student acting as the messenger, bringing me in to be molested.

It happened so often that I eventually realised it would never stop unless I put a stop to it. For the second time in my short life I would have to confront my abuser.

One morning, when I knew Mr X would be in his office, I decided that it was now or never. I stormed into his office without knocking, something that was expressly forbidden to students.

He looked up, but his expression barely changed. Just a flicker of annoyance across his face.

'Robinson,' he said mildly. 'Get out.'

'Fuck you,' I said, as calmly as my anger would let me. 'I'm going to the headmaster and I'm telling him everything.'

At that, he turned pale. He scrambled up from his desk as I spun on my heel.

The whole way to the headmaster's office, Mr X followed close behind me.

As I approached the office, my heart sank. The headmaster's personal secretary was just on her way out of his office, which she was only permitted to enter when the headmaster was not in.

I hammered on the headmaster's door a few times, but it was not to be. The office was empty.

Mr X grabbed me by the arm and dragged me down the hallway until he found an empty room. He pulled me into it and sat me roughly down on a chair.

'This is what's going to happen today,' he hissed. 'If you ever tell anyone what has been going on I will tell the other boys that you came on to me. I will let them know you were abused by your grandfather, and that you liked it, because you're a little pervert.'

He also threatened to tell the staff he'd caught me stealing from lockers and other students' bags, and that I'd been hurting and abusing animals in the animal nursery.

In the short term, he said I was banned from playing sport, and that I'd have detention with him every day until 5 p.m. until my grades improved.

Mr X opened the door to the hall. I got up, shaking badly, and made to walk away. He followed closely, yelling loud enough for anyone to hear: 'What's it going to be, Robinson? What are you going to do?'

It felt like it took forever to reach my locker. I quickly shoved all my belongings into my bag, walked to the bike rack, and rode away, Mr X's mocking voice still ringing in my ears.

It took me years to realise that none of that was my fault. He had identified me as a damaged boy in need of care, and therefore a potential victim. The kindness he'd shown me was actually him grooming me. He was one of countless paedophiles enabled and empowered by schools and the church.

But I had instantly decided I would not be setting foot back in either school or church. My childhood, in every practical sense, was over.

As I rode away from TSS, my tears dried. I headed straight to the streets of the Gold Coast, which would be my new home. There, I knew the rules. There, I could take care of myself – on the street, I would become top of the class.

11

Going viral

In late 2018, a reporter from the Gold Coast gave me a call.

'I've heard the strangest story about this bloke going around crashing funerals,' he said. 'Is that you?'

'Mate, sounds like something I'd do,' I replied.

So we got to chatting and he wrote up a story about the funerals I'd attended as the Coffin Confessor. It was originally intended as a human-interest story for the local news, but it went online and suddenly people from all over the world were reading it. I had gone viral.

In the days after the story went online, the newspaper was inundated with calls from people asking to be put in touch with this 'Coffin Confessor'. In the end the journalist called me and asked if he could just give out my number.

From all the requests that came through, there was one in particular that captured my attention: a nurse to a young man dying in a Brisbane hospital.

Thomas Gillis was barely thirty, and he was going to die. Not only was he going to die young, he was going to die horribly. He had bone marrow cancer, which every doctor I've ever spoken to says is the most excruciating pain you can go through on your way out. The last thing Tom would ever see was the inside of a palliative care unit. Shit that's grim.

If you've ever visited palliative care, you'll never want to do so again. Walking through the halls of the hospital on the way to this meeting, I was shocked by how many people there were to a ward. There were usually only one or two people to a room, but the whole ward was full. And everyone in there knew that they were not ever leaving.

I couldn't shake the thought, *Wow, the length of this corridor – that's the end of their life for all these poor people.*

Some had a window looking out onto the city and could maybe watch the shadows move across the building next door as the day crawled by. Most didn't. Some got a mirror that reflected the corridor so they could keep an eye out for nurses coming in with morphine – or see the beds roll by as the deceased were moved from the ward.

It's no way to die. None of that is the nurses' fault, of course. Being a palliative care nurse must be the hardest job in the world. Those men and women are trying to do the best they can in a deeply unfair situation.

Tom's nurse was a great bloke. He'd more or less become Tom's best friend in those final days, someone who could still make him laugh. They were close enough that when Tom indicated he wanted me to crash his funeral, the nurse stepped up and put the wheels in motion.

Tom had been a fun-loving guy all his life – very friendly, very active, really into extreme sports. That's actually how he'd found out he was sick: he'd been out mountain biking, come off his bike and hurt his leg. He took a routine trip to hospital to get the injury checked out and while he was there they noticed something wrong with his lymph nodes. They took him in for further tests and discovered he had leukaemia. In the course of treating that, they found the cancer had spread to his bone marrow. There was nothing to be done.

If he'd never come off his bike, they never would have found it. He might have spent his final months in blissful ignorance, rather than going through desperate, painful and ultimately futile medical treatment.

* * *

Tom's mum and dad were shattered, naturally, although they didn't let it show. They were very reserved people, conservative Christians, from a denomination that was very traditional in its views, especially around family.

It was their belief, for example, that a woman's place was in the home, specifically in the role of mother. The mother was taught to know her place and remain deferential to the men in the family at all times. Not really my thing.

This is what gets to me about some branches of Christianity. They worship Mary as a deity, make a woman one of their key religious figures, but then don't see women as worthy of equality on earth? What's that about? I've a low tolerance for bullshit and hypocrisy in any organisation, and a lot of the time churches are overflowing with both.

Now and again, I'll get someone who thinks I'm committing sacrilege when my client requests an interruption to a religious service. 'How dare you! A priest is God's voice on earth. Did God give you permission to be rude to a priest?'

'No, God didn't tell me that, but did God tell all these priests to rape all these children? Or commit literally millions of murders in his name over the years? I don't fucking think so. I don't believe in God, but if there is one, I'll have some words with Him when I die.'

That tends to shut them up.

Yeah, religion does a lot of good in the world. But it's done a metric fuckton of bad as well. No amount of faith gives you the right to shove it down someone else's throat.

I have no hesitation standing up in a church and telling a priest to go fuck themselves. It's actually very satisfying. I recommend it for any survivor of Church-affiliated child sexual abuse. It's healthy – an act of self-care. Like eating your broccoli, or jogging. Except it's refusing to give a cleric the moral authority they sacrificed when some of their brethren decided they wanted to touch children.

My wife, who is somewhat religious, doesn't love that part of my job.

'What if there is a God, Bill?'

'What if there is?'

'Well, you're going to meet your maker one day. What happens if you're standing in front of God and he wants to know why you told his priest to go fuck himself?'

'I'll tell him, "Same reason you let your priests rape, humiliate and torture generations of women and children. Now can I pass through the pearly gates? Yep? Have a nice day."'

* * *

But live and let live. I don't have any right to tell you your religion is wrong. What do I know? I'm an atheist, but that doesn't make me right.

This branch of Christianity was what Tom believed in, and it seemed to bring him comfort in his final days. But that religion, with its taboo against public displays of affection, was what Tom needed the Coffin Confessor for.

His folks weren't into showing love and affection, no matter how loving the family might be, and this is why Tom had hired me. His whole life he'd wished his family could be more communicative and show that they loved each other. Little things like hugs and telling your parents you love them had never been part of his life.

The way he told it, Tom had always hoped that with time their relationship would change to become more demonstrative. Now he was out of time. All he wanted was to declare to the world, publicly, that he loved his parents, and to know that they loved him back. He'd tried a few times in his life, especially after he got sick, but he always broke down and found himself unable to get the words out.

Now it was late in the day for Tom. He was on end-of-life palliative care, and only conscious for minutes at a time.

That got to me, I must say. I found it terribly sad. Not so much that he was dying so young – I'd seen plenty of people who were younger than me die. Street kids on drugs, young men hanging themselves in jail, guys beaten to death in front of me. Death comes for us all; it doesn't really matter how many years you've had. I'm fairly tough to crack that way, I guess.

No, the thing that got to me about Tom's request was how simple it was, and how pure. All he really wanted was a hug from his mum and dad.

I took the job, for a fraction of my usual fee.

* * *

The funeral was attended only by a small group. Looking around, it was clear that Tom didn't have many close friends. Some business associates, a strong showing from his religious community, but I could identify nobody who might have been his best friend, or his lover. It was the sort of funeral you have when, in life, you've never really had the opportunity to express love for other human beings.

I waited for a pause in the proceedings, at which point I stood up, excused myself, and announced: 'My name is Bill Edgar and I am the Coffin Confessor. I've been engaged by Thomas Gillis to say what he couldn't.'

I opened the envelope and read aloud what Tom had left unsaid.

'To those of you here at my funeral, thank you. I love you. Please help and support my mum and dad. Love always, Tom.

'To my mum and dad – Mum, Dad, no parent should have to outlive their children, but the life you gave me was full to the brim. I doubt I could have fit any more love inside it, or me. Thank you for being there by my side and please never forget that I loved you both as much as you loved me. I'm no longer in pain and will always be with you, so please don't cry over me, or be sad for too long. It's not healthy to grieve forever, and we now know that our health is far more important than anything else.

'Mum, Dad, I have left instructions with the Coffin Confessor to hand each of you an envelope. In it is a gift from me to you both. Please enjoy it, and think of me as often as I will of you both. Your son, Tom.'

I put the letter back inside the envelope and placed it on top of the coffin.

I wanted, if I could, to really bring Tom's final request to life. I wanted to make it understood that he loved his parents more than anything in the world, and that this love was more important than any shame they might have felt about expressing it because of their culture or community.

It was really unfortunate – you could tell the love was there, and it was real. I would have done anything for that kind of love when I was a child. That made it even more bittersweet to see the pain it put Tom through. Not everyone gets to have a family, and some people will never know that kind of love.

Before I left, I handed over the individual letters Tom had written for his parents, who took them without meeting my eye. Then I was gone.

12

Not your average street kid

I went straight from TSS to the streets of Surfers Paradise, on the Gold Coast. They were safer for me than school or my mother's house, which was saying something, because the streets weren't exactly very fucking safe.

But at least I understood the rules there. They were simpler than in the shifting, morally ambiguous world of the TSS elite. On the streets, it didn't matter who your parents were – you found your own way to survive. If you weren't the biggest, you had to be the fastest. If not that, you had to be the smartest.

Street life was tough, degrading and traumatising, which left you vulnerable to all types of people. There was no guidebook, and if there had been it would've been too expensive to buy, and not worth stealing, since it wasn't food or money.

For most kids, it was a life without a lot of hope. But not for me. Life on the streets is what you make it – and I made it my home.

* * *

I knew that living on the streets didn't mean that I had to do the same thing as every other street kid. There was no reason I had to become an alcoholic or drug user with no future or ambition. I was different to most, and this attitude led me to living a very comfortable life, in relative terms. I was always warm in winter and cool in summer. I hardly ever went hungry. I taught myself how to survive and grabbed every opportunity that tried to pass me by.

The first week was terrifying. I was a traumatised kid with an empty stomach, sleeping in parks and public toilets, one eye always open for predators. After a few freezing, restless nights, I started to figure some stuff out.

I would sit and wait behind bakeries at 3 a.m., when the bakers threw out the previous day's stock of cream buns and Vegemite scrolls. Garbage to them, but a feast to me.

One morning I noticed the milkman delivering milk to the front doors of houses and I decided to follow him. At first I tailed him from a distance, grabbing the odd bottle of milk and sculling it while it was still ice-cold. Then I realised that some houses left payment for the milk in envelopes under their empty bottles, so once I had learned his route I ran ahead and stole that money. I used it to buy hot pies and pasties once the shops opened.

When it got cold, I jumped fences and stole clothes straight off people's Hills hoists.

Then I learned about the untapped goldmine that was the Gold Coast theme parks' lost property departments. I'd jump the fences and go straight to the lost property counter, where I claimed jumpers, hats, sunglasses, wallets – whatever I could find. It was like a lucky dip.

'Hello!' I'd say cheerfully. 'I've lost my watch. Can I have a look at any that have been handed in?'

It turns out you can steal almost anything if you put your mind to it. The biggest thing I ever stole was a whole Gold Coast unit, fully furnished, with power and running water.

Walking past a unit complex, I noticed a big rental agency sign in a window. I put my face to the window and peered through to get a better look at the unit. I realised the window was unlocked, and I was able to slide it open and climb inside without anyone on the street noticing. Inside, the place was ready to go for some happy sea-changer – lounge set, bed, desk, even a television.

I looked around for anything worth stealing, and had just opened the door to make a quick getaway, when a neighbour happened to walk past and introduced himself as Frank.

'You must be the new bloke,' said Frank. 'I'll show you where the fuse box is so you can get your lights and fridge on.'

I had no idea how a fuse box worked, so he showed me the switch to power up my new home. Then he asked me if I needed anything else.

'No thank you, Frank,' I said. 'I should be right from here.'

That night I fell asleep on the couch, watching TV, more than a little chuffed with myself.

The next day I went out shoplifting and picked up some bedding, a toaster and some cutlery, making my new house a home.

I ended up living there for just over three months. One day a real estate agent – a nice young lady – knocked on the door and told me she was there to inspect the place. When she asked who I was, I told her I was the tenant, renting privately off the new owner. She seemed confused and unconvinced, but luckily these were the days before mobile phones, so she said she'd go and check with her office then come back to see me.

After she left I knew I had maybe fifteen minutes to get what I needed and get out of there. It took me five. I was gone, back on the street. Easy come, easy go.

* * *

The Gold Coast and Surfers Paradise, where I lived, had no shortage of street kids and poverty, but it was crammed up next to incredible wealth. There was this really prestigious area called Paradise Waters. Nearly every waterfront home had a jetty leading down to the water, where rich people kept their boats. I knew from the kids at TSS that most of those yachts were hardly used – only taken out on the weekend, if that – so in my eyes they were basically floating hotel rooms.

I'd watch them for a little while to see if someone was on board, then slip aboard and into the cabin. Half the time they were unlocked, but even if they weren't, it was easy to gain access. Then I would feast on the minibar, helping myself to whatever I could find: little bottles of booze, tinned food, crackers, fancy antipasti and smallgoods. I would put my feet up and sleep on clean sheets, making sure I was gone by sunrise, cleaning up any trace that I'd been there and leaving the place pristine, so that I'd be able to go back and raid it again a few weeks later.

The couple of times I was caught I managed to escape by diving overboard. One guy was really furious, and I think he would have killed me if he'd gotten his hands on me.

Another time the bloke must have seen me breaking into his boat from his house up above. I was just settling in to stay the night when I heard a deep man's voice call out. 'You, in the boat. I know you're in there.'

I froze, ready for flight or fight, but he told me that he'd left something to eat. He said I should make myself at home, but not be there in the morning. Sure enough, when I crept out to look, the guy was walking off, but he'd left me a plate of hot food, kept warm under foil. In the morning, I disappeared, but not before spotlessly cleaning the boat and washing the plate.

* * *

Once I got the hang of the streets, I could usually find somewhere to sleep. For a while my favourite spot was the cinema. It was safe and warm, and I could sneak in during the last session, hide under the seats, and then after all the staff had gone home I could stretch out on the floor to sleep.

There was usually food to be found between the seats too. A packet of Jaffas, half a box of popcorn. I loved popcorn – the problem was, so did the rats that swarmed the place after dark. That first night, I woke up with them all over me. They'd come for the popcorn littered on the floor, and instead found me on their dinner plate: 'Awesome, let's chow down on this dude.'

It was fucking rank. At first I hated them, but after a while I got to know them and made sure to sleep out of their feeding territory. I made a game of following them, trying to work out where they lived, but they were too fast and too secretive. They'd be running up and down with bits of popcorn in their mouth.

To this day, I still admire rats. Smart as shit, they don't give a fuck about anything but living their best life. It's pretty inspirational when you think about it: born survivors, they know how to get by on any street in the world.

I could get into most places just by visiting during the day and hiding out until closing time. I went to Sundale shopping centre – the only massive shopping centre at the time – and walked around while people were shopping, then hid in the middle of the clothing racks and waited until the store closed. Then at night I crept out and made myself at home. There was a lone security guard patrolling the centre and I'd wait for him to go by, then run down to the other end of the shopping centre.

There was a little boutique in the centre that sold gourmet food and there I ate like a king, stuffing my face with champagne ham and chocolate truffles, all that shit that was the height of sophistication in the eighties. When it was time to sleep, I found a nice cushy area with plush carpeting and made myself a little nest out of clothes from the racks.

Other nights I'd break into supermarkets and feel like I was a lost boy out of *Peter Pan*. Imagine being a street kid with an empty stomach and here's this incredible sight: rows and rows of food. I learned how to walk up and down the aisles of stores without triggering the sensor lights or the alarms. I made myself a feast and curled up in the warmest place, and always cleaned up after myself.

None of these places were safe to crash in for more than a few nights, though. Someone always worked it out and chased me away.

* * *

For quite a while I made my home in a bowling alley. One night I was sitting around town, waiting for it to get dark. Off in the distance I could see a man shutting down a bowling alley for the night, turning off the big neon sign and locking up a sliding glass door. He looked around and, thinking the coast was clear, hid the keys behind a loose brick in the wall.

After he'd driven off, I walked up to where he'd been standing. After a long search, running my hand along the wall, I found the loose brick. Pulling it out revealed a little hiding spot and a set of keys, which I quickly grabbed, replacing the brick before anyone saw me.

I peered through the doors into the building. In the dim light I could just make out the alleys, shoe counter and soft-drink machine. But it's what I couldn't see that was most important: no sign of the blinking lights that indicated security cameras or burglar alarms. Jackpot.

The first thing I did – what I always did in an unfamiliar place – was look for a way out. I could never relax until I'd worked out an exit strategy. It's been this way my whole life. You never know when you'll need to get out of a situation in a hurry, and I always make sure that I know about a back door.

Once I'd worked out a potential escape route from the bowling alley, I wandered around sipping soft drinks, eating potato crisps and chocolate. That was my dinner most nights back then – no matter where I ended up crashing, I always managed to find chips and chocolate. A few years earlier, when I'd lived with my mum and went to bed with my stomach growling most nights, I would have done almost anything for a block of chocolate, but I got sick of it pretty quickly. These days, chips and chocolate remain two of my least favourite things to eat.

I loved that bowling alley though. There was a bar upstairs called the Chevron Hotel, and just off the staircase that led up there was a little crawlspace that stayed warm all the time, and where no one went during the day. Inside that crawlspace I made a little home – a sleeping bag, a little light, some food. It was awesome; no more park benches for me. I had comfort, warmth, food and sleep.

I was always entrepreneurial – there's opportunities everywhere, you just have to look in places nobody has ever thought to.

* * *

Summer was better than winter. It made it much easier to stay clean, which was important to me – nearly as important as finding food. I felt filthy, still unable to look in the mirror without feeling disgust for what my grandad and teacher had done to me. I hated my body, hated my skin. The only time I felt a little relief from that shame was right after I'd showered.

Back then, I would have three showers a day if I could. That was never easy while I was sleeping rough, but it was at least a little easier when it was hot enough to jump into the surf – I found the ocean very cleansing – and then rinse off under the public showers on the beach.

Then I discovered surfing – quite by accident. I had broken into a house near the Broadwater and was eating out of the fridge when the residents came home unexpectedly. I escaped through the backyard. As I was about to jump the fence, I found a surfboard leaning up against it. I tucked that under my arm and went over the fence. Using that surfboard, I jumped into the canal and paddled across the water to safety.

I went all the way down to the beach and jumped straight in the surf, then paddled out on the board to cool it out on the ocean until any trouble on land calmed down.

Luckily the waves weren't too big that day; I just watched the other surfers out on the waves and imitated them until I got the hang of it. It took me a little while to get the hang of standing up on the thing, but after that I was hooked.

It was one of the few times during that time when I felt at peace. I'd go out past the breaking waves and just bob there for hours, all alone, completely anonymous, just another guy out on the ocean. There, my past didn't matter. It was like being in a little bubble, bobbing this way and that on the waves.

* * *

I had learned to drive the same way I learned to surf: I stole a car and worked it out.

It wasn't a hard thing to do, stealing cars. Movies had taught me that it was this stressful, complicated procedure of hot-wiring the ignition and sparks flying all over the place, but that turned out to be total bullshit. On older vehicles, you just take a screwdriver, bash it into the ignition, turn the handle, and the car is yours. Couldn't be easier. A child could do it. In fact, a child taught me how – another kid showed me the ropes.

Other street kids would break into cars, take them on joy rides and really fuck them up. Even if they didn't crash them, they'd deliberately vandalise them when they were done: smash the windows, piss on the seats. I thought that seemed quite rude, and I only stole a car if I needed to get from A to B. I'd jack it, drive to where I needed to be and park it somewhere they'd be able to find it – untouched, except for the screwdriver in the ignition.

I would have never stolen a thing if I didn't have to. There are a few things I did back then in order to survive that I regret now.

But then again, because of the way I'd been brought up and the experiences I'd had, the lines between right and wrong were blurred beyond repair. Nearly every authority figure I'd ever known had betrayed, humiliated or abused me. How was I supposed to have respect for the rule of law? I did what nearly every street kid seemed to do back then – I stole to survive.

It's not an easy life. The consequences hit you hard and fast. Often literally.

At sixteen, I was tasked by this guy, Matty, to get his motorbike from Brisbane to Surfers. Matty was a guy who had an incredible ability to make friends with – and coerce – the most dangerous fucking people. Most of his business was drug related, and he was a bad guy to cross. So when he asked me to pick up this bike, I accepted the job.

The bike was a brand-new GSXR-1100. It went from nothing to eye-watering speed in seconds. Of course, it was stolen. And of course, on the outskirts of the Gold Coast, the cops spotted me and tried to pull me over.

When I noticed the flashing lights behind me, I panicked. Nervous, unlicensed, on a stolen bike, on a highway in broad daylight, I didn't know what to do. So I hit the throttle.

The cops hit the sirens and sped up to run me down. I couldn't shake them – I would get away from one car and then another one would appear. Soon I had three cars on my tail, sirens blazing.

So I went faster, pushing the bike up to 180 km/h, leaving the police far behind.

I watched them fade in my rear-view mirrors and felt invincible, hurtling down Frank Street, towards Surfers Paradise. Soon enough another police car was trailing behind me, but I had to slow down to cross a bridge. I squeezed the brake, coming down to 130 km/h, then 120 km/h. I pulled in the clutch to tap on the gear pedal and drop down to third gear. The problem was, this was one of my first times on a motorbike; without realising, I tapped all the way down to first gear. I released the clutch at just over 100 km/h.

The crash was an out-of-body experience. It was just like when I was being abused, when I would drift away from my body, watching what was happening but feeling nothing. I heard the horrible crunching scream of gears jamming inside the bike, and then I was thrown off, flying through the air while the bike skidded on its side.

I remember hitting the ground and rolling over and over, until I came to a stop on the side of the road, staring up at the sky. I was wearing nothing but jeans and a singlet, but somehow I'd avoided cracking my head.

I stood up and checked myself for damage. I wasn't hurt at all. No broken bones, no blood, not even any pain. I just stood there, wondering how I'd gotten away without a scratch on me, when the police car that had been chasing me just sped by as though I wasn't even there. They hadn't seen me go down.

I had to get away from the scene and the wrecked bike, but thankfully I knew the Gold Coast better than most. On every street there were places I could hide, sleep and eat without anyone knowing I was there.

Most importantly right then, I knew my way around the sewer system. The Gold Coast is built on a network of stormwater drains, which I used to get from one suburb to another without being noticed, and I wasn't far from the entrance to one of those drains.

I was running towards it when I heard more sirens closing in. Suddenly, I had a better idea. There was an industrial-sized bin nearby that several businesses in the area used and kept unlocked. I lifted the lid, climbed in, and burrowed into the trash, covering myself with a piece of sheet metal.

Not long afterwards, I heard commotion outside – footsteps running in every direction, the crackle of a police radio. I distinctly recall an officer standing just outside the bin, telling dispatch that he'd followed my footprints towards the stormwater drains, and to send search teams down there.

I lay in the dark, sweating and shaking. I heard police searching the area all around me. I knew it was only a matter of time before they thought to search the bin, but I didn't dare move in case they caught me trying to sneak off.

Suddenly the lid to the bin opened. It had been broad daylight when I climbed into the bin, but I could see stars in the night sky. I must have fallen asleep and not realised it. Or maybe I'd hit my head after all.

The lid creaked open, and a familiar face leaned into the bin. It was an old man who lived on the streets, always carrying a hessian sack for collecting scraps.

I was so relieved he wasn't a cop, I shouted in delight and started to scramble out. The old man startled to the point of dropping the lid again, nearly knocking me out for the second time that day.

Once I was out of the bin, I dusted myself off, nodded politely at the old man, and walked off in the direction of Surfers Paradise.

It seemed to me I really was invincible. I was so jacked up on adrenaline that my feeling of invulnerability lasted for three days. Then I finally started to bruise all over my body and realised I was actually in quite a lot of pain.

I wasn't invincible after all. Just very, very lucky.

* * *

Of course, even the best luck doesn't hold forever.

One day I got a little too brave and decided to steal a car from the local service station. It wasn't a very flash car, just a beat-up little sedan, but as I passed I saw the driver had left the keys in the ignition while he went in to pay for his fuel.

On impulse, I jumped in the car and drove away. A perfect crime, except for two details. One, the car was a manual, which I had no idea how to drive; I stalled it trying to change gear a hundred metres down the highway. Two, the driver was surprisingly fast on his feet, despite being the biggest Samoan bloke I'd ever seen in my life.

He caught up with me in a flash, opened the car door and dragged me out onto the road. The first punch broke my nose and after that I was paralysed with fear. I couldn't feel anything, even though he hit me again and again.

After a good beating, the guy let me go. I lay in a heap by the side of the road while he got back in his car and drove away. He only got a couple of hundred metres up the road before I saw the car stop and the reverse lights come on.

My first thought was that he wasn't finished, that he was coming back to give me another hiding. Instead, when the car stopped beside me, he threw a spare shirt at me.

'Here,' he said. 'Wipe the blood off your face, bro.'

Then he climbed out of his car, sat down next to me and explained why he'd beaten me so badly. He said he was frustrated – he was on his way to a job he hated, and he had to work double shifts because his wife was pregnant.

'I've got no money. I could only afford to put five bucks' worth of fuel in my car, and now some little prick wants to steal it.'

'I'm sorry,' I said through the blood-soaked shirt I was holding to my face.

He shook his head. He told me 'sorry' was just a word for someone who doesn't have control over their life. It was no good seizing an opportunity if it was going to disadvantage someone else. My actions could ruin someone's day, or their life, and I wouldn't even know it. Or worse, I might find out later after all, and get my nose broken for the trouble.

'Nobody owes you anything, least of all me. I've got nothing to begin with.' He got up and opened his car door. 'I hope this has taught you a lesson, bro. God bless.'

I watched him drive off down the road until his tail-lights disappeared. I felt terrible.

Life has a way of kicking you in the guts when you're down; I had stolen a car off a guy that was in more need of help than I was, and he had a job and a family.

I hated myself for what I had done, and after that I became more selective about what I stole and who I hung around with, trying to better myself each day. Whenever possible, I asked shopkeepers for work, or offered to work for food, only stealing as a last resort.

* * *

One night I started a fight with a complete stranger, for no reason other than I wanted to. He was bigger and older. Much like stealing that car from the servo, he taught me an important lesson. It would be the last time I picked a fight for the fun of it.

This guy knocked me on my arse before I could even throw a punch, not once but three times. Each time, I got up more determined to beat him, only to go straight down again.

Eventually he stopped the fight by putting his hands down. 'Enough, bro.'

After that, we got to talking. We actually got along pretty well. He told me he trained at a boxing gym not far from Surfers, and suggested I turn up and get into boxing.

So for a minute I thought I'd try a career as a boxer.

I strolled into the boxing gym and sort of announced, 'I've arrived. I'm going to be the best boxer in the world.'

And this grizzled old boxing trainer went, 'That means you've got to train, you know? You can't be a boxer if you don't train.'

'It's simpler than that,' I argued. 'I get in the ring, beat the fuck out of the other guy, and then I'm the champion.'

The trainer just walked away, shaking his head.

He allowed me to fight a few times, and I always won, but he would explain to me that the way I was fighting wasn't actually boxing – which he thought of as this elegant sport – but brawling.

'You can't bite people, Bill,' he told me. 'You're not allowed to scratch or kick. You can't try to rip someone's ear off.'

'I won, didn't I?' I'd protest.

'Winning isn't everything.'

It was to me, though.

One day I sat down and did the maths. I realised that all the best boxers in the world endured years of pain, taking a couple of hundred fights to come up through the ranks, with no money and no titles, before they got any real reward for their sacrifice. I didn't want to fight a hundred guys to get a cheque – I wanted to fight one and walk away a champion.

Plus I saw firsthand how badly it can fuck your body up. A lot of those old timers don't do so well after retirement.

I decided then and there that boxing wasn't for me.

In these elite boxing gyms there was no money for aspiring champions, but there was a bit of cash put aside for people they could practise on. So after getting to know the trainers a bit, I'd go in and be a sparring partner for well-known boxers.

I figured I could try my hardest to be a professional boxer and get paid in nothing but trophies, or I could get punched and make money. It was a no brainer. I was like, 'Just hit me a few times and give me some money.'

I'd found the perfect job for me: human punching bag! Easiest money I ever made. All I had to do was stand there – ducking, weaving, blocking, throwing the occasional shadow punch – while the next big thing in boxing darted all around, smacking me with jabs.

The only problem was occasionally they'd land one I wasn't expecting and I'd react without thinking and knock the poor guy out.

'Sorry,' I'd say, bending down to help them up. 'I thought you were meant to be a professional.'

It was good while it lasted.

13

The queens of Ipswich

One lesson I've learned the hard way, again and again, is that good things don't last forever, so you should enjoy them while you've got them. And celebrate the time you had once it's gone.

Sometimes a funeral can be a joyful thing. Rather than dwelling on everything you've lost in a loved one, you celebrate the time you had together. Joseph's funeral definitely fit into that category.

Joseph had hired me to crash his wake and make a few announcements. The bloke was a bit of a character. He and his boyfriend, Brian, were known around town as the queens of Ipswich. They had been together for years, and called each other husband long before gay marriage was legalised in Australia.

Really outgoing and flamboyant, they didn't give a fuck what you thought, and nobody was going to stop them having a good time. It's worth emphasising how much guts it took for two men to live as an out couple in the era when Joseph and Brian were young. All through the eighties and nineties, street kids and teenagers on the Gold Coast would go out 'poofter-bashing' for something to do on the weekend. It was a deeply intolerant society in that way.

With the prejudices my generation grew up with, the propaganda against homosexuals – and gay men in particular – made them out to be no different from paedophiles. The way I grew up understanding it, there was no difference between my grandad – a paedophile and sexual predator – and blokes who just happened to be into other blokes. As I grew and became more educated, I realised how ignorant that thinking was. Same-sex love is just love, it's that fucking simple.

Joseph and Brian were always the life of the party. In his day, Joseph had been the sort of guy who was always coming up with new inventions. Certain ideas he'd come up with along the way had made him a great deal of money, and he and Brian had lived a very full life.

They were always looking for something quirky they could do for fun, something a bit out of the ordinary. So when Joseph knew he was dying, he figured he may as well make an event of it. They hired the Coffin Confessor more or less as a special guest, a five-minute novelty.

I've got to say, that was a great funeral. It was my job to turn up, make a little speech and then hand Brian an envelope. I don't know what was in that letter, but it made Brian really emotional. For a few minutes he just stood there, holding the letter to his chest, with tears rolling down his face. Happy tears, but not without a great deal of sorrow too, I think.

I'd been asked to tell everyone to have a nice time, and to inform Brian he should check the sock drawer when he got home.

On Joseph's instructions, I'd already prepared the scene. There in the sock drawer, on top of the neatly arranged rows of socks and jocks, was a fresh box of condoms and a short note.

'Goodbye now,' it said. 'Have fun and be safe.'

14

My extraordinary ordinary wife

I honestly did always just want a normal life. A roof over my head, money in my pocket. Someone I could put my trust in and not have it blow up on me.

More than anything, I wanted to go to school. I wanted an education, and craved the company of people my own age. The kids I was running the streets with were all a little older, and hardened by what they'd been through. They were great to have around if you needed to steal something or bash someone, but they weren't exactly what you'd call mates.

Sixteen years old, bored and lonely, I was walking past a backyard and saw a Southport State High School uniform spinning around on the Hills hoist and nicked it. Dressed in the uniform, I walked into the schoolyard and found some kids who looked around the same age as me.

'What year are you guys in?' I didn't even know what grade a boy my age was supposed to be in. 'Year 10? Alright, that sounds good. Where do I go?'

They told me they were on their way to maths class, and showed me that they had diaries and timetables that told them where to go. All of this was new to me; I had no idea how a regular school worked – at TSS everything had been built around it being a boarding school – but I followed the kids to class.

I went in and introduced myself to the teacher as a new student. She told me she wasn't expecting anyone new, but it was no problem.

'Take a seat. Try over there.' She pointed across the room.

Sure enough, there was a seat free in front of a pretty blonde girl, who was staring at me. I went over, sat down and sort of tried to act cool by leaning way back in my chair. But I leaned too far back and bumped the desk of the girl behind me, sending books and pencils scattering everywhere.

I was trying to keep a low profile and doing a shit job right away.

'Seriously?' said the girl behind me. 'What are you doing?'

'Sorry,' I said, drawn into her beautiful blue eyes and pretty much falling in love straight away. I'd never seen someone so beautiful.

Her name was Lara. For a few months we hung out together, just as part of a larger group, until one day I finally asked her out. I felt I'd chosen my moment perfectly and was expecting her to say yes immediately. Instead, she took a long pause after my question.

'I suppose so,' she said eventually.

A few months after that, someone at the school realised I wasn't actually enrolled as a student. I'd have to stop turning up to class. But by then it was too late – Lara and I were in love. Technically, we were high-school sweethearts.

* * *

Lara was a good girl; a fine student and a gun athlete. Milky white skin, long blonde hair and very broad shoulders. She was a swimmer, on her way to becoming an Olympian. She was being trained by former Olympian Robbie Nay, and she was touted as the next big thing in swimming after Tracey Wickham and Lisa Curry.

Every morning and afternoon she was in the pool, doing laps, shaving microseconds off her personal best, getting better and better. She was breaking records even back then, and still holds a few school records that have never been beaten.

I was clearly a different sort of kid. Lara always said I had potential, but I couldn't see it in myself back then.

The closest thing I had to stability was my own car – a Ford Falcon XB I'd bought from two brothers, Tony and Kermit Coe, for $250. I knew Tony from my work as a human punching bag, and Kermit sold the best foils of weed.

The XB became my home. I used to park at the service station around the corner from Lara's mum and dad's house, sleep there at night, then wash myself under the tap you're meant to use to put water in your radiator. Then I'd get changed into my cleanest clothes, pick Lara up and take her out for the day.

Not everyone was thrilled about our romance. Lara's older brother, by coincidence also called Scott, said he was going to break my neck. He used to chase me all over the Gold Coast, and I'd have to run as fast as I could to get away.

And her coach, Robbie Nay, fucking hated me. Truth be told, I didn't much care for him either.

Robbie told Lara that she could do better and that she was destroying her chances of becoming an Olympian by being with me, but she wouldn't hear of it. She wouldn't stand for anyone saying anything negative about her new love. When those around her tried to drive us apart, it only widened the gap between her and those who loved her.

Looking back, what her family was worried about was exactly what was happening: she'd fallen in love with a lost boy. And I'd fallen in love with this perfect young woman. It was a classic case of opposites attracting.

I ended up stealing Lara away from her entire life. I desperately needed stability and love, and she wanted to love me as a way of fixing the damage from my childhood. Because I'd never had any attention or love, I craved it badly; I would never be able to let her go.

All of a sudden, this girl was my entire world.

Lara inspired me to change – to try and course correct. I told her about my past and what had happened to me, and she was the first person to ever offer me comfort and help rather than taking advantage of me. She encouraged me to try to reconcile with the past. She helped me find out who I really was.

While trying to get money from social services to get a place for the two of us to live, I learned my real name. The clerk who was trying to help me couldn't find a Scott Robinson that matched me in any government records. Mum had never bothered to change my name legally, she'd just told me I was Scott one day. It was this clerk who told me my real name and gave me a copy of my birth certificate. I was William Scott Edgar.

I had already known that the boy known on the streets as Scott Robinson was not good enough for Lara. That day, I decided it was time for Scott Robinson to die.

With the little money I had in my pocket, I walked into a second-hand store and bought new clothes. New everything: shorts, shirts, underwear, even a pair of thongs. Not so much earlier I would have stolen those clothes, or better versions of them, but I was done with all that now.

I walked in, stripped off naked, and left the identity of Scott Robinson in a pile on the floor with my old clothes. From then on I would be William Edgar – Bill for short – and I would have nothing to do with any of the Robinsons ever again.

* * *

I tried to do my best by Lara, but my existence was still precarious. Survival was very much a day-to-day thing. When I finally got enough money together, we found a unit and moved in together. And then she told me she was pregnant.

Back then, my best mate was aghast. He was like, 'Run!'

But I was horrified by that reaction. 'Why would I run? I love this chick. I'm going to have a kid!'

I was so excited! Fucking hell, I had no idea what we were in for. The way holding your child for the first time rewires your whole brain; your thoughts, perspective and entire existence rearranges around them.

At the age of eighteen, Lara gave birth to our son. Although I'd spent most of my life in danger, I never understood what real fear was until I had a child. The fact that we'd brought this life into the world, and now it was my duty to nurture and protect it – it was profound. I would have done anything for my son, endured anything. I was prepared to change my life entirely. Little did

I know, my life was going to be changed for me very soon. Some very bad shit was just around the corner.

* * *

When I was living on the streets, I'd become part of a community of street kids. We'd go out and find a way to survive the day, then at night we'd sometimes group together in a park or under a bridge to make beds for the night. The cops hassled us a bit, moved us on, but it wasn't a big deal.

Some of the cops were genuinely decent blokes. If they caught you up to some mischief, and they could tell you were genuinely a street kid who was hungry and desperate – escaping a bad situation somewhere – then they'd give you a kick up the arse, or a clip on the ear, and send you on your way. They knew that most of us were just trying to get somewhere safe and warm, or get a feed.

There were exceptions, of course. Some of the other kids saw crime as a way of life. A couple of guys I hung out with had ambitions to be proper gangsters. These kids, Ben and Zac, were always trying to recruit other kids into a gang that they could be the head of. They got up to proper criminal shit. Bashing people up and taking their wallets, which they called 'rolling' them. As in, 'Let's roll this guy!' They stole cars and stripped them down for parts, selling what they could.

None of that for me. I hated vandalism and I hated gangs. Couldn't stand the thought of being in one. They used to say there was safety in numbers, but not for me. I was better off alone.

Looking back, these guys' efforts to get a gang started and

make street life into a business was really fucking naïve. It was never going to work.

It was enough to throw me into the shit, though.

One day, when I was still only sixteen, we rolled this guy for his smokes. We didn't even want them – we were just looking for trouble, really. I asked for a smoke and he wouldn't give me one, so I started giving him a hard time, for no reason except I wanted to be a smart arse.

It didn't seem to me like a big deal, but he went to the cops, and their response was completely disproportionate to the crime. Police from all over the coast converged on us. It was a manhunt!

They caught us under the highway bridge that runs across the Nerang River. One minute we were just hanging out, then suddenly there were cop cars coming from all directions.

They arrested us and threw us in the back of a paddy wagon, and Ben started freaking out.

'Oh, we're fucked now. We're going to get done big time.'

Zac was trying to keep his cool. He had this really serious expression and kept telling us, 'Say nothing. Don't tell them a fucking thing.'

'What's the matter? Relax,' I said. 'They've got nothing. We stole some smokes, big fucking deal.'

We got to the watch house, and they put Ben and Zac in one cell and me in another. I wasn't worried at all. At sixteen, I was sure that as a juvenile offender I was going to walk out and get off scot-free. I didn't realise that in Queensland, in the justice system you're considered an adult at seventeen, and my birthday was right around the corner. You might not be old enough to buy a beer, but in the eyes of the law, you're old enough to serve time.

I found this out soon enough. A cop came up to me and asked me if I knew what I was being charged with.

'I stole a cigarette.' I shrugged. 'Big fucking deal.'

'What about your mates? How well do you know them?'

I told him that they were just street kids like me. 'We hang out, find food, whatever. I don't really know them that well.'

The cop just shook his head.

'Well, you know they're bank robbers? There's a warrant out for them. Armed robbery. And you're going to be charged alongside them.'

'What's that?' I blinked at the cop. 'For what?'

'You've been arrested under the Crimes Act, Section 99. "Demanding property with menace, with intent to steal." But since you'll be standing in the same dock, the prosecution is going to go you for armed robbery as well. You're looking at eight to twelve years.'

Well, shit, I thought. *Got that wrong, didn't I?*

* * *

I was remanded in custody in prison. With no home or money for bail, the judge thought it would be best if I was held until trial.

So for three months I sat there in my cell, trying to figure out what I was going to do. I watched other people come and go – the cops dragging in new arrests, the old ones shuffling out. Now and again a lawyer would come through to talk to their client, but never for me.

Three months passed. My seventeenth birthday came and went unmarked as I sat in that cage. But in that time I got to know the patterns of the watch house, and before long I began to recognise certain lawyers. One day I saw a lawyer, Wallace, who I knew by reputation to be a great bloke, one of the rare lawyers who actually gave a shit.

I called out to him. 'Hey mate! Can I see you for a minute?'

He came over and I told him the situation. He advised me that if I were to stand trial with Ben and Zac, it was very likely that we would all be charged and convicted for the bank robbery. I would do the same time as them.

He sort of lowered his voice and said, 'Between you and me, you do not want to show up in that courtroom under any circumstances. Make of that what you will.'

Wallace said he could get me out of the watch house on conditional bail. That meant I would have to go and live with somebody, so if I could give the police a name and address – any name and address – he could get me out until my trial.

I gave them my uncle's name and address. He had no idea, but luckily they didn't seem to check with him. I got bail. I was allowed to walk out, on the understanding that I would appear in court two weeks later, to stand trial with my co-accused. That meant I would effectively be tried for armed bank robbery for the crime of stealing a cigarette. So of course, when that day came, I was miles away.

It was the smartest thing I'd ever done. One of them got six and a half years in maximum security, the other nine. Turns out Zac and Ben had each spent their whole remand period giving the prosecution evidence to use against the other. Honour amongst thieves – what a bullshit idea. Maybe that holds on the outside, but in custody, for blokes like them, honour is just another currency to be traded away.

Of course, after that, there was a warrant out for my arrest, for failing to appear in court. Wallace had advised me to turn myself in, but no way was I doing that. I didn't give a shit. I would just keep running the streets forever.

Not long after that, naturally, they nabbed me. I was in the park, just putting together a bed for the night out of boxes and other shit, when the flashing lights came on.

The cops were just doing their regular routine, kicking people off the street. If they found you in a park, they'd tell you to find somewhere else to sleep and move on. But I was in a bad mood; I told them to fuck off. They arrested me, found I had a warrant out, and that's how I ended up with another three months in jail.

I got three months for the initial crime, three months for skipping court, and they added a little extra time for a break and enter.

That was an incident where I'd broken into the Anglican Church where the pastor I'd met through my friend was serving. One night I passed by and thought of the time I'd confided in him about my abuse – how he could have easily saved my life, but instead shamed me. So I broke in and trashed the church as revenge. But it came back to bite me on the arse once I was in the justice system.

I had just turned seventeen, still only a kid, but they sent me to Boggo Road, a colonial-era prison so notorious for cruelty and brutality that they would shut it down in 2002. These days they run ghost tours of the place.

The truth of the matter is, I reckon they put me in there because there was nowhere else to send me. I had nowhere to live, no work, no food, no money. Lara had gone home to live with her mum and dad. Prison isn't just for criminals; it's a dumping ground for the poor, the mentally ill, the disabled, anyone who society doesn't know what to do with.

That was me. I was a street kid living on whatever I could scrounge, scavenge or steal. It was always only a matter of time before I ended up in lock-up, but in the end, after all the shit I'd done to stay alive – stealing cars, breaking and entering, selling drugs – I was arrested for stealing a cigarette.

How funny is that? One cigarette. I didn't even smoke! Suddenly I was locked up with some of the hardest, most violent, deviant sexual predators on the planet. And there I was, like, 'Hi, guys. I stole a cigarette, what are you in for?'

It was fucking terrible.

* * *

But you know what? That's not even the worst news I got that month. During the couple of weeks after the trial, before the cops tracked me down, I slept and hid out in an abandoned factory no more than 50 metres away from the Southport Police Station.

One day, while I was heading back to the factory, a small silver car pulled up next to me. I was about to leg it, but then I saw it was my mum and one of my aunts. They got out of the car and asked how I was.

'I'm fine,' I lied. Even if I was going to prison soon, I didn't want to worry them.

Mum seemed unconvinced. She asked if there was anything I wanted to tell her. I took this to mean that she'd heard I was in trouble with the law. I was trying to decide what to tell her when my aunt interrupted.

'What your mum means is . . .' she seemed to struggle for the right words. 'Did Grandad ever . . . touch you?'

I stared at her in shock. This is not something I wanted to talk about with them. It was too embarrassing. I couldn't believe they'd asked me.

'Yes.' I was surprised to hear myself say it. 'I tried to tell you for years, Mum. You never believed me.'

I told my mum everything, and demanded to know why she never defended me.

'You would get angry and hit me whenever I spoke badly about Grandad.'

She didn't answer. In fact, she didn't say anything at all. Her and my aunt just walked back to their car and drove away, leaving me standing on the street like a lost puppy.

I felt sick, angry and hopeless. I arrived back at the abandoned factory, curled up in a ball and cried myself to sleep.

After a few days, I decided to call around to my mother's place, where she still lived with my sisters and brother. But when I got there, I found that they were in the midst of packing up their belongings. They were getting ready to move house yet again.

I found Mum in the kitchen and asked if she needed any help packing, and where she was moving to. I was hoping that, wherever it was, it might be big enough for me as well. She looked me right in the eye and told me she was moving in with my grandad.

I'm sure my heart skipped a beat; I found myself struggling to breathe. So many thoughts and emotions ran through my mind – I couldn't really understand what she'd just told me. Just a few days ago I'd confirmed that her father, my grandad, had been abusing me for years. Now she was moving in with him.

That's when I started to put it all together. The fishing trips with Grandad she'd sent me on. All the times she'd put me into a room with him alone. The way she'd beaten me into silence whenever I tried to work up the courage to tell someone.

She'd known. She'd known all along.

The worst part of all was the money she took from him, the handouts he gave her so she could keep living her life without ever working a day. My own mother had sold out to a paedophile. Not just any paedophile, her own father.

When the abuse was at its worst, there were eight adults in a three-bedroom house. I wondererd how they couldn't know what was going on?

Years later I had all this confirmed by other relatives, but it was at that exact moment that I lost all feeling and respect for my mother. Where I'd once had love, and the lonely hope that she would love me back one day, there was nothing, nothing at all. It all left me, every bit of feeling for this woman. It just vanished, never to return.

In the moment, in that kitchen, I was angry in a way I'd never felt before. I wanted to spit in her face. But something else took control of my actions and, before I knew it, I was headed out the door without another word.

She was dead to me. Whatever prison had in store for me, it couldn't be worse than what had come before.

15

Final request

I've got a number of Coffin Confessor clients who have hired me well in advance. Some of them aren't anywhere close to the end of the road – young people in fine health. They just want a little insurance, maybe. To know for sure that their final confession won't follow them into the grave.

They'll give me an envelope with their secrets in it and move on with their life, knowing that I'll read it out at their funeral. Part of the deal is that the specifics of the secret remain sealed in that envelope until after their death.

In my office, I've got envelope after envelope of secrets. I never read the letters until the time comes for me to do so at the funeral, but usually, before I agree to take on a job, I'll have some idea of what to expect.

Some funerals I've crashed have been parties, others have been bittersweet, but a few have simply been non-events. Some people lead the sort of life that means nobody is there to see them off.

When those people hire me, it's because they are holding on to deep-seated, horrific regrets. The sort of secrets that ruin other people's lives.

A couple of times I've sat with people as they've told me how they want their funeral crashed and something about them has made my skin crawl. One guy disclosed to me, basically, that he'd done some bad shit in his time. He was sexually deviant in the worst way – he was into cruelty, voyeurism, bestiality. That was just the tip of the iceberg, I think.

He was a real piece of shit, especially where his family was concerned. Essentially your run-of-the-mill abusive partner and dad, mentally and physically terrorising his children. As a result of that, his daughter had died, and the rest of the family no longer had anything to do with him.

Whatever else he had to confess beyond that, he'd given to me in an envelope to read to the assembled mourners at his funeral.

Truthfully, I was dreading it a little bit. I can't say I was looking forward to whatever this guy had to get off his chest post-mortem.

On the day, I turned up early and waited. And waited. Nobody came – not one soul.

The priest did his little boilerplate speech to a row of empty chairs. When that was done, I got up, put the envelope on the coffin, and walked out. My job was done.

If our task in life is to lead the sort of life that means people give a shit if you live or die, the deceased had failed.

* * *

Then you've got people who slip between the cracks in society, usually through little fault of their own. There are so many people who reach the end of their lives having been used, abused and then tossed aside by everyone who was supposed to care for them.

Judy had nobody in the whole world. She was one of those people who have just been completely abandoned. If, once upon a time when she was young and beautiful, somebody had cared for her, they were no longer around. Now there was nobody. She was a professional 'massage therapist', who worked in the rub-and-tug establishments of the Gold Coast and was well-known in the seedier hotels along the strip.

A former drug addict, although she was fifty-three – just a year older than me – she looked to be in her eighties. She had rehabilitated herself and gone clean late in life, but she retained that jittery energy that some former drug addicts carry with them long after recovery.

Her body was ruined by intravenous drug use and the diseases that can come with that. Emphysema, heart problems, calcified veins, blood clots. On top of all that, she now had terminal cancer. She didn't have long to live.

When she knew she was dying, she started to worry about what to do with her ashes. She'd found out that when you die without next of kin and with no money for a proper burial, you become the responsibility of the city council. You are summarily cremated and, unless someone volunteers to collect your ashes, they are scattered in the gardens of public land.

Judy hated this idea. Certain experiences in her life had made her terrified of the idea of becoming a ward of the state, even in death. But without a friend in the world to collect her ashes, she didn't know what to do.

That's how she found me. She was online one night searching the internet for what came next: 'What happens when you die?'

'I was googling all sorts of stuff,' she told me when we met. '"What's the afterlife like?" "What are the alternatives to being put in the ground to rot?"'

Judy had looked at all sorts of options, and for a while she'd considered one of those planter boxes where they bury your remains along with seeds, and in time your body decomposes and nourishes a tree as it grows. In the end, though, she decided she wanted to be cremated.

'I want to go into the ocean. Don't mind where,' she told me. 'I'm a Pisces, a water sign.'

Apart from that, her requests were very simple. She wanted me to interrupt her funeral service and tell the priest to sit down and shut up, as she was an atheist and had no room for organised religion pretending it cared about her once she was gone. After a lifetime of bullshit, Judy didn't need any more.

Her life had been too hard for her to suffer fools now. In that way, I could relate to her. People will tell you that we all make choices and that we deserve to be where we end up. Well, sure, but some people never get a choice. Some people are forced into those choices. Human beings aren't fucking produce to be put in a basket and sorted by type.

She'd lived on the street. She'd had to beg, borrow, steal. I know what that's like.

She had the body, she could sell it, and that allowed her to make enough money to survive. There's no shame in that. There's dignity in survival – much more than in judging someone else against your own idea of a moral life.

I felt for Judy, I really did. If I hadn't had the good fortune of meeting Lara, who saved me going down that route, who knows where I'd be now. Judy owned fuck all in this world, but I wasn't about to insist on my usual fee. I agreed to do the job.

Judy had survived for half a century, even if all she had to show for it was her memories. She had this belief that you should try everything you can whenever you got the chance. That you should make as many memories as you possibly can while you're alive, because they're the only things you'll take with you.

She didn't want to share all those memories with me, because some were too precious to her. She wanted to treasure those herself in whatever afterlife she found herself in. Kind of like a glory box she was keeping for the next world.

What she did want to tell me about, endlessly, was her clients. The celebrities who'd frequented her hotel room. The local politicians who, during the week, campaigned for conservative political parties, and then on the weekend paid her to do BDSM sex shit. The married men that frequently visited her and used the opportunity to confide in her. She reckoned she was part hooker, part therapist; she knew these men better than their own wives did.

That was her final request of me: that I let the clients who'd shared her bed every so often know that their secrets were safe. And to buy them a round of drinks. She had a thing about buying drinks for people. It was one of her great pleasures in life, to shout a round and be shouted one back.

So, after the funeral, I picked up her ashes. One lovely morning shortly after, I scattered them into the waterline at Main Beach, just outside of Surfers Paradise. I said a few words; it was just me, Lara and my dog.

Afterwards, I went to one of the hotels where she'd been well known when she was doing sex work. It was the middle of the day, a quiet time for the pub, just a bored bartender and a table of tradies in high-vis. I wondered if any of them knew Judy, as a client or a drinking buddy. Would any of them miss her? Or even notice that she wasn't around anymore? If they did, would they give a fuck?

As per Judy's final wish, I bought them a round of beers and approached them at the table.

'This beer comes courtesy of Judy Jackson,' I announced. 'She's now dead, and she's taken your secrets with her.'

They were a bit taken aback, but thankful for the beer.

'Cheers!' they said, toasting Judy Jackson who, true to her word, had moved on from the world with nothing but her secrets.

It was very sad, the whole thing. There are so many people who are just never given a chance at life. They are undone by abusers all the way through, gaslit and stunted. Judy was just one of them – there's a billion more in the world. Most of them end up in the same place, and that's not a place you want to be.

16

Boggo Road

I'd escaped a high-speed police chase on a stolen motorbike, punched on with professional fighters, but that was nothing compared to day one of prison.

All my senses were working overtime. I could hear, see and smell everything and everyone. Every detail in perfect clarity. At the same time, I was trying not to look at anybody directly, or let on that my legs were shaking uncontrollably.

As they loaded me into the prison van, the hyperreality of the moment really sunk in. I could feel it in my bones. This was it. I couldn't run, hide or escape from danger. All the tricks I'd been using to stay alive – my wits, my speed – none of that did me much good chained to the seat of a prison transport van.

There were eight other inmates in the van, all different ages and backgrounds. Three of them were returning to prison after attending court, the rest were first-timers like me who'd just been given their sentence. I was the youngest of them all. One of the old-timers gave me the once over and then addressed all us newbies.

'You know what you got to do to get respect in jail, don't you? You've got to go up and hit the biggest bloke you can find. Make a stand, make a statement from day one.'

The other two convicts burst out laughing, but they agreed. Me and the rest of the new blood were left freaking out. What on earth were we in for?

The truck slowed and stopped at the gates of the prison. We could hear the guards asking how many prisoners were on board – their ages, names, logistical details like that. Then came the screeching metal-on-metal sound of the Boggo Road gates opening up.

Boggo Road Gaol is notorious around the country. It was Brisbane's main prison from the 1880s until the 1980s, when I was unfortunate enough to do my stint there. By then it was infamous for poor conditions, rioting, hunger strikes, persecution of prisoners, and violence.

The prison was divided into the colonial-era Division One and the more modern, but equally brutal, Division Two. If you lived there, they were known as One Gaol and Two Gaol. The official name for both yards was Brisbane Gaol, but everyone called it 'Boggo' – the prisoners, the police and even the prison guards, the screws, who ran the place.

Why were they called screws? It's a very old slang term, back from when the guards would literally turn a screw to lock the yards up. It didn't hurt that they were always trying to screw us prisoners, in one way or another.

The truck rolled on into the yard and came to a stop. We could hear the gates screeching closed again behind us, then the truck was unlocked and we prisoners were unloaded. We were directed to stand along a yellow line painted on the sealed road, where a roll was called.

A prison officer stood in front of us calling out names off a list. When your name was called, you were supposed to say 'Sir!' and salute. I was waiting my turn when the prisoner to the right of me, also a newbie, decided to take his first bit of prison advice as gospel. Without warning, he punched the biggest guy he could see.

Unfortunately, the biggest guy around was a prison officer, who stood about six and a half foot and easily weighed 120 kilos. It was a good punch, though, and dropped the giant guard to the tarmac.

Screws came running from everywhere and jumped on the guy who'd thrown the punch, beating him with batons.

Scared that I would be dragged into the melee, I started to move away, but the prisoner to my left grabbed me by the wrist.

'Don't move,' he hissed.

I listened, and we all stood stock-still as the screws laid into the bloke on the ground with clubs and boots until he was unconscious. After he stopped twitching and was dragged away, the rest of us were left to stand around staring at the blood on the ground and contemplating what had just happened.

I turned to thank my new friend, who was looking at me with a serious expression on his face. He advised me that prison was a dangerous place, especially for such a young, fresh-faced kid, and warned me to be very careful about accepting help from others – each time it happened, I would incur a debt.

I nodded and told him I'd take his advice on board.

'Smart boy!' He smiled. 'Now give me your shoes.'

Shocked, I looked down at my feet. I was wearing a nice pair of sand shoes. I liked them, but I hadn't considered that they'd be taken from me, or that they'd be something anyone wanted to steal. Not that I had much choice, as I saw it. This bloke was probably going to get them off me anyway, and spilling more blood on the bitumen wasn't going to achieve anything.

Even as I took them off, I tried to argue. 'They won't even fit you. I'm a size eleven,' I protested. 'You look like a thirteen.'

He grinned and told me they weren't for him; he wanted them as a present for a lady friend. With that, he headed towards his yard, carrying my shoes, while I wondered what exactly he meant by 'lady friend' in a maximum-security men's prison.

Have you ever had that nightmare where you turn up to the first day of school, or a new job, and realise you've forgotten to get dressed? That's how I felt standing on the hot bitumen of Boggo with no shoes and no idea how I was going to survive the coming months.

I was feeling more than a little vulnerable when a prison officer asked me my name and date of birth. After he had ticked off my name, he told me to follow the yellow line to reception. There I was processed, strip-searched for contraband, and then directed to take a shower and get my prison uniform.

I noticed that prisoners, not guards, were working behind the counter where they handed out the prison clothes. Fellow convicts handled much of the basic clerical work in that place. These guys' official job was to make sure we were properly attired. Unofficially, they were there to haze and intimidate us newbies.

As they handed over the clothes, they ogled and wolf-whistled the pretty young prisoners, letting them know how good-looking they were, and how popular they would be in the shower block. They thought it was hilarious, having a great laugh amongst themselves.

When it was my turn to collect my clothes, I stared straight into the eyes of the prisoner making most of the jokes. He handed me my prison clothes and said, 'Have a nice stay,' as though I was checking into a hotel.

I thanked him politely, and turned away to head into the changeroom, but he called out to me.

'You're not going to get far without shoes. Here, these will fit you.'

He threw me a pair of new shoes. I don't know why he was so kind to me.

* * *

Our prison-transport truck had left just after breakfast, and not long after we'd finally been assigned a yard and a cell, the meal siren sounded. We were escorted into the main dining hall. All of us newbies stood there with our chests puffed out and our faces stony, trying not to make eye contact with anybody, but also trying not to look like we gave a shit if we did.

I knew that my body language would naturally dictate how I was perceived. If the bullies and predators of Boggo Road sensed I was afraid, it would make the coming months very unpleasant. This was complicated by the fact I was shitting myself with fear.

I couldn't help but feel intimidated by the rows and rows of prisoners. The sight of so many criminals in one room was overwhelming. I got the distinct feeling that all eyes turned to look at me. In fact, this wasn't paranoia – they *were* all staring at me. In hindsight, they were probably just inquisitive about the new prisoners they would be living with, because not much happens in prison to break up the boredom. But of course, to me, it felt like every hard man in that room was sizing me up.

I picked up a tray and joined the line slowly shuffling along the serving counter. Once I had my food and turned to take in the room, my hands were shaking so badly that the cutlery rattled on the tray.

This was the most terrifying moment of all: finding a seat.

The prison population is extremely self-segregating, and the dining hall was like a diagram of all the groups and cliques, separated by race and creed. Each table seated ten individuals of one tribe or the next. One table might be all Vietnamese guys, another all Pacific Islanders. Indigenous Australians here, skinhead white-supremacists there. Gangs, too, including bikies, the Hunters and Rebels guarding their own tables.

I had to sit somewhere. What a fucking choice. I wasn't in a gang, nor did I want to be in one.

I went up to a random table with an empty seat. There were two big fellas – one with teardrop tattoos on his face and another with spiderwebs tattooed all over his shaved head. Just as I went to sit down, Teardrop casually threw his arm over the back of the empty chair, all the while keeping one eye on me to gauge my reactions.

I understood that this was a situation that would affect the way I was perceived as both a person and a fellow prisoner. My actions in this moment would define how I was treated for the rest of my stay in prison.

The way I saw it, I had a couple of options. The first was to accept this and walk away in search of another vacant seat. But by doing this, I'd be showing weakness, signalling that I was easily told what to do and when to do it. That was not something I wanted, especially in a prison environment.

The second option was to ask Teardrop to remove his arm so I could sit in the vacant chair. But if he refused, I would either have to fight him or walk away and still be marked as weak.

The third option was to pull out the vacant chair regardless of the arm wrapped around it and take my chances. I figured this could be detrimental, as other prisoners might interpret it as bullying behaviour, which carried the risk of getting me into more fights than I cared to be in.

In the end, I went for option three. I pulled out the chair, put down my tray, and sat down to eat.

'Can't sit here,' Teardrop said, staring at me.

'Relax.' I stared back. 'I'm just going to eat my lunch and go.'

Teardrop grabbed my tray and slid it across the table towards himself. There was a tense moment, then I grabbed the tray back. This went on a few times, back and forth, until the tray spilled off the table. You only got one feed, so that was me done for lunch. But truth be told, I had thrown up in my mouth from anxiety so many times that day, I didn't need to eat.

Mealtimes were pretty uncomfortable those first few days. Then on the fourth morning, after I'd just grabbed my breakfast tray, Teardrop came up and smacked it out of my hand.

'Alright then,' I said, squaring up to fight. 'Let's fucking do this.'

Teardrop waved his hands to calm me down. He explained that he was helping me out. The breakfast I'd been holding was full of shaved glass and had been intended for another prisoner.

Breakfast was always disgusting – either beans on toast or scrambled eggs reconstituted from powder – but the blokes in the kitchen would make it worse by either jerking off in it or shaving glass into it. If you happened to get your food alongside a prisoner who'd been marked as a target, there was a good chance you were going to get the contaminated breakfast meant for him. Teardrop didn't like me, but he didn't want me eating glass meant for someone else.

After that, I never touched the scrambled eggs again. I only ever ate toast for breakfast. And after I made it clear to a few of the standover artists and would-be toilet-block rapists that I wasn't one to back down from a fight, everyone was reasonably respectful and didn't mind where I sat in the dining hall.

The rules in prison are basically the same as they are on the outside. Don't touch what isn't yours, have respect for other people's space and circumstances, and never judge anyone with any criteria except your instincts. If you follow your gut, most times you won't be placed in a situation where you feel intimidated, even if it's just taking a seat to eat lunch.

* * *

One of the hardest things about prison was the routine of it all. Ever since I was small, I've found I can hardly bear to be still, so to sit and do nothing all day was a kind of torture. Some prisoners are content to sit around and stare at the walls all day. Not me. I needed something to do or I was going to go crazy.

After a little while, when I'd learned the lay of the land, I was given a job as a runner. That's one of those jobs that only exists in a prison. Basically, a prisoner was given permission to roam the prison freely so they could deliver messages to and from prisoners in different parts of the jail. It's a job that requires permission not just from the screws but also the top dog of the inmates. As such, it's not a job to be taken lightly. If you fuck up, retribution is going to come from both the law and the criminals.

As a runner, I was able to move between One Gaol and Two Gaol, passing along messages to friends, brothers, gang members, whatever. People would write them on a scrap of paper, then I'd fold it up and hide it in my mouth. If I was stopped and searched by a guard who wasn't in on the deal, I was to swallow it. At first the messages came thick and fast. I never read any of them, figuring it was none of my business. I was just happy to have something to do.

The job gave me free rein of the jail, and earned me the respect of the prison powerbrokers. Once a runner had gained the trust of both the prisoners and the guards, his life was significantly more exciting than your average inmate's.

It was also a valuable source of income – prison wasn't a cheap place to be. Inmates on good behaviour had the option to work menial jobs, doing the laundry and such, but the pay was abysmal. Ironically, crime was the only way to make life comfortable.

The busiest time of the week was always buy-up day, when prisoners were able to purchase coffee, tea, biscuits, cigarettes and other items from the prison store. Your family and friends could put a little money into your account with the store.

Back in the eighties, we were given free smokes – two pouches a fortnight of a tobacco called Flagship, an orange pouch with a picture of the *Endeavour* on the front. They sold normal cigarettes at the shop.

I learned very quickly that if you bought those cigarettes, especially Winfield or Marlborough, that was gold to a lot of people. I could use them to barter for pretty much anything.

Buy-up day was also when most debts were settled. For soft targets, it was a day of extortion. I quickly learned what, when and how to order, and to keep my finances to myself. If word got out that you had money available, then someone much harder and scarier than you would make you an offer – pay them protection money or expect to be bashed, raped, and bashed again.

I personally had very little money, but my work in the prison earned me enough to purchase tea or coffee to last the fortnight. I was always sure never to be indebted to anyone; I had seen first-hand what happened to those that didn't pay their debts.

In my time in prison, of course, the 'messages' I was delivering usually weren't just Christmas greetings or invitations to lunch. Running contraband was a large part of the gig.

A guy in One Gaol might come up to me and just spit something into my hand. 'Deliver this to Jimmy in Two Gaol.'

That was that. I'd have to put it in my mouth, and if I got caught, swallow whatever it was.

I'd trot over to the other yard and Jimmy would be there waiting for me – fuck knows how he already knew to look for me – and I'd spit it out into his hand. Then he'd swallow whatever it was and get a buzz.

It was tablets, mainly, but half the shit was liquid, in these dodgy little packets. LSD, codeine, speed, heroin sometimes, and all sorts of crazy synthetic substitutes.

A couple of times I was stopped by the guards and was forced to swallow whatever it was. What I didn't realise was that anything you swallowed, you had to pay for.

The first time I had to go back to the guy that hired me and let him know that I got stopped, he said, 'Well, then you owe me, don't you?'

'How am I meant to pay?' I complained. 'I don't fucking have anything but someone else's shoes.'

'Give me your shoes, then. Or a tin of Milo. Whatever you've got, you've got to pay.'

'Okay, okay.'

That meant I had to go out and make more runs to pay for debt incurred on the last one. Using what I earned, I slowly traded up. A pack of smokes for a tin of Milo, then a dirty magazine, and so on, until I'd built this sophisticated portfolio of prison-currency bullshit.

That was lucky, because it turned out I'd walked into Boggo Road with a major debt that I'd incurred on the outside. One day in prison, I ran into my old mate Matty, the Gold Coast drug-dealer whose motorbike I'd crashed. He was in Boggo for some serious violent crimes, and he was none too happy to see me. It took some fast talking, and some even faster money, to get back in his good books. Being a runner of messages definitely helped with situations like that.

But then of course I became known as the guy who could get you shit. I just wanted to keep my head down and do my time, but all of a sudden everyone was like, 'Oh hey, there's the Road Runner. Where you going, little fella?'

And I'd just wave hello, my cheeks full of fucking horse tranquilliser or whatever, jogging off to see a man about it.

Now and again I'd have to swallow a package and get high as a kite. One time I just collapsed right in the middle of the yard and a screw had to come scrape me off the floor.

'What's wrong?' he demanded. 'What are you doing?'

'Just . . . you know . . . enjoying it.' I laughed.

'Enjoying what?'

'Oh. Just, you know . . . the weather.'

'You're a fucking nutcase.' The guard shook his head, letting me go. 'Fuck off then.'

The guards knew what was going on, of course. How do you think all that contraband got into the prison in the first place? But you never knew which guard was in on it and which wasn't. For that reason, it was a dangerous job. If you got caught with a little bag of smack by the wrong guard, suddenly you had another couple of years on your sentence.

But I enjoyed it. It was just the gift of the gab; I certainly didn't have any other assets I could leverage in there. I could fight, sure, but there's always someone tougher than you, or at least willing to fight dirtier.

Being a runner was a good job to have in prison, but it was far too easy for me to end up in over my head. So I decided to stop.

I approached the prison chief on duty and told him my running days were over, but after that I still had to get the all clear from the top dog in the prison population, Jimmy. Jimmy was tall and muscular, but quiet – the sort of calm that let me know I was dealing with a truly dangerous person. When a bloke doesn't need to act tough in prison, you know he's someone you shouldn't cross.

I approached Jimmy and told him that my running days were over. He listened, thought about it, and suggested that I finish out the week. He was very persuasive. I decided that one more week of running was a great idea after all.

* * *

Prison is a place where the lines blur, getting fuzzier the longer you stay inside. Through tension, attrition and hard-earned respect, prisoners and guards learn to work together. Occasionally the distinction between screw and inmate gets hazy.

Prisoners form gangs, and those gangs form hierarchies. They develop complex, socially accepted ways of behaving around other prisoners, with old-timers keeping the peace and settling disputes amongst young hotheads.

The guards, too, formed their own traditions and acceptable codes of conduct. In any other world many of these would be considered amoral – and in a place where they didn't have almost total authority, they would certainly be illegal.

I knew of one screw whose favourite thing in the world was a prison riot, because it gave him an excuse to get out his shotgun. I overheard him once explaining to another guard that the trick to shooting a rioter in cold blood was to aim just in front of his feet. That way you could take out the rioter's legs with the ricocheting pellets and still plausibly claim that it had been a warning shot.

Keep in mind that prison is awash with contraband: drugs, weapons, and in the modern era mobile phones too. In a maximum-security facility like Boggo Road, where every visit is supervised and comes with a free strip search, there's no way that the sheer amount of illegal goods flowing through the prison population gets in without the blessing of the guards. The guards make a tidy profit to supplement their wages, and the prisoners get their hands on what they need. The more influential a prisoner, the more they can arrange to have smuggled into the prison.

I happened to be in Boggo Road at the same time as the stick-up artist Wayne 'The Horse' Ryan. Ryan was serving eleven years for a series of armed bank robberies. He'd earned the nickname 'The Horse' because he'd successfully done a runner and escaped from Boggo Road the previous year. Now he was back inside, but his notoriety made him something of a prison celebrity, and he had the ear of more than one of the screws.

One day I was working out in the prison gym. A prisoner I knew quite well, a Kiwi named Ivan that I worked out with now and again, came over to me.

'Bro. You've got two choices. You can run and not stop to look back, or you can lie down on the floor and stay out of the way.'

'Mate,' I said. 'What the fuck are you talking about?'

He shook my hand, said that he'd always liked me and told me to take care. Then he headed towards the prison laundry, which was just near the gym.

I was baffled, at a loss as to what he could possibly be on about. Looking around the gym, there didn't seem to be anything out of the ordinary going on. I stuck my head outside the door, and it was business as usual out there too – the laundry truck being loaded with dirty sheets and uniforms to be taken away, a handful of prisoners exercising on the oval.

I went back to my workout, convinced that my Kiwi friend had finally cracked under the pressure of prison life and was talking nonsense. Seconds later, I was lying on the floor with my hands over my head. Gunshots echoed through the jail.

The alarm started ringing, and in the hallway I heard shouting and then the low rumble of boots thudding by as guards rushed towards the laundry. Then I heard the roar of the laundry truck starting up, and seconds later a god-awful crash of metal on metal. I got to my feet; those of us in the gym looked at each other wide-eyed. *What the fuck is going on?*

I moved to go out and have a look, but a guard holding a large plastic riot shield and a pistol ordered us all back onto the floor.

We waited, under guard, until the gunshots stopped, and then finally the alarm too.

A prisoner who worked in the kitchens stuck his head in the door and I asked him what had happened.

'The horse has bolted,' he said with a smile.

It turned out that Wayne Ryan and seven other prisoners had used handguns to hijack the laundry truck, which they then used as a battering ram to get through the prison gates. It was a major news story in all the papers the next day, and extremely embarrassing for the prison.

All prisoners were confined to their cells after the escape, and many of us were brought in to be questioned about any knowledge we had of the escape plan. I personally don't think anyone knew anything. To get a gun inside could only mean one thing: it was an inside job. A prison guard had helped them. For all we knew, one of the guards demanding to know where Wayne Ryan had got the gun was the one who had brought it in for him.

Everyone has a price, and for most screws that price was pretty low. Pay the right guard the right amount and they will look the other way on almost anything. Most were more than happy to make themselves scarce at the right time, especially when a score needed to be settled between prisoners.

* * *

Violence was very much a part of prison life. The guards would bash a prisoner at the slightest provocation to send a message about respecting their authority. Other inmates would come after you with their fists, or with shivs and other improvised weapons so horrifying you didn't know whether to be afraid or impressed by the ingenuity.

A simple toothbrush can be deadly in the right hands – a prisoner could spend countless hours rubbing the handle against a concrete floor to sharpen it into a shiv. With a razor blade from a disposable shaver and some tape, you could make a little axe just large enough to quietly slit someone's throat as you passed them in the yard.

Jail introduced me to some of the most unspeakable acts of violence imaginable. Some of it didn't even require the perpetrator to lay a hand on their victim. As well as mixing glass shavings – off the bottom of a drinking glass – into someone's scrambled eggs, they'd put them in their victim's toothpaste. They hid razor blades in bars of soap, so you wouldn't notice them until you started scrubbing and ran them over your skin.

These acts were particularly popular to inflict on inmates who had been imprisoned for crimes against children. Paedophiles, called 'rock spiders' by other prisoners, were particularly reviled. They were the lowest of the low in the prison hierarchy.

One wet and windy day, while waiting for service at the buy-up counter, I noticed a group of eight prisoners being escorted from one part of the prison to another by just as many prison officers. I thought to myself that meant those guys must be dangerous, and that I should steer clear, but then all of a sudden the prison erupted into chaos. Prisoners from all over the common area stood up, shouting abuse and threatening the prisoners being transferred, while the prison guards formed a protective perimeter around them.

I asked the guy in front of me in the line what was going on.

'Rock spiders,' he spat. 'Scum of the earth. Kiddy fiddlers.'

I saw red. Back then, I had a lot of trouble controlling my anger towards paedophiles. Sure enough, these were prisoners who were deemed to be security risks – they would be in danger in the general prison population. Paedophiles and crooked cops were often targeted by vigilantes.

In this case, one of them was both.

David 'Officer Dave' Moore was an officer in the Brisbane Police Department's public relations unit throughout the eighties. He appeared on popular children's television shows like *Super Saturday* and *Wombat*, where I remembered him appearing alongside Agro, the puppet, and warning children about stranger danger. He was later busted with child pornography and sentenced to prison for having sex with a sixteen-year-old boy.

It just so happened that a few days after seeing him across the yard, I ended up in the same room as Officer Dave.

Because I was only seventeen, I was kept in Two Gaol, which was the more heavily policed area of the prison – the same area the protected prisoners were housed in.

I'd been called to the reception area, where I was told to take a seat and wait for my name to be called. Next to me sat another prisoner. He just stared into space with a blank look on his face. Without looking at me, he spoke in a low voice.

'Mate. Hey, you. You know who that is sitting over there?'

'No, and I don't give a shit.'

'He's that copper. You know the one – off the kid's show. The cop who played with children.'

I understood what was happening. Someone had arranged for me to be in proximity to Officer Dave so that I could bash him. That sort of thing happened all the time in Boggo Road. As I said, a guard could be bribed or a favour called in to give one prisoner the opportunity to have a crack at another one. Because I was in the same area of the prison, and because I had made no secret of my burning hatred of paedophiles, it had been arranged for me to take care of this one.

When someone higher up in the prison hierarchy wanted you to bash someone, there was normally some reward in it – cash, drugs, even just stuff from the store. I'd seen people beaten to a pulp over a tin of Milo. That was just how it was.

There were consequences if you refused to bash somebody, too. One hard man I knew who refused to follow through on a prison hit was bashed for his pacifism, and gang-raped for good measure.

But to tell you the truth, I would have gone after that fucking paedophile cop for free. He was there on TV, warning kids not to talk to strangers, even while he was molesting them himself.

I looked at the prisoner sitting beside me. He smiled and gave me a nod. In a strange way, that smile is what drove me to action. If he hadn't smiled, I wouldn't have done a damned thing.

Officer Dave took one elbow to the head and hit the ground. I only had time to get one more hit in before the screws reached me, but believe me, it was a good one. As the guards dragged me away, the prisoner who'd pointed out Officer Dave laughed.

'Bro! You give a shit now, don't ya!' he called out to me.

His laugh echoed all the way to the room the screws took me to. They beat the shit out of me. They used their batons to take my legs out from under me and then worked me over until I was a mess of blood and bruises.

The screws were careful not to break any bones, though; they needed me healthy enough for what came next. They dragged me out through the yard into solitary confinement.

17

H.M.C.

In late 2018 I got a call from a woman down in northern New South Wales. She said she was a carer for a gentleman at the end of his life and she'd heard about me from one of the mourners at Christine's funeral, where I had confessed Christine's love for her best friend.

The woman who called me said she had a patient, Rod, who had been very sick for a long time. He was miserable, but after she'd told Rod about me, he cheered up immensely. He had certain regrets, she'd told me, including one or two major things that he wanted to put right, now that his time on earth was over.

'Alright,' I said. 'I can help with that.' I asked where the gentleman wanted to meet me, and the carer elaborated on the situation.

'What,' she asked me, 'do you know about bikers?'

* * *

The Hunters Motorcycle Club are a half-century-old, old-fashioned outlaw motorcycle club. They're 2000 members strong, and divided into regional chapters all over Australia. If you're not familiar with the Hunters, you've probably seen them pop up on the news, brawling in an airport or heading into court flanked by lawyers for some drug, assault or weapons charge.

The Hunters rarely speak to the media, and when they do they maintain that they are simply a fraternity of big blokes who love big bikes and hanging out together, enjoying the finer things in life.

The cops see things differently. For decades they've gone after the Hunters, alleging they are a sophisticated organised criminal organisation and behind all manner of nasty, illegal enterprises. The Gold Coast chapter, in particular, have long been a target of law enforcement.

In efforts to shut them down, over the past couple of decades governments around Australia have pushed through a series of dodgy laws. The most extreme of these were in Queensland, where in 2016 the so-called bikie ban made it the first jurisdiction in the world to ban the public display of motorcycle club colours, restrict biker gatherings, ban club members from opening certain businesses, and ram through mandatory jail terms for biker-associated crime.

When these laws came into effect in Queensland, more than one gang member had to leave the state. This included my new client Rod, who was a sworn, colour-wearing, Harley-riding member of the Gold Coast chapter of the Hunters.

These days Rod was living in exile out the back of a small town, the best days of his life in the rear-view mirror. He didn't have long to go, and he was dying across the border from his Hunter brothers, to whom he'd pledged his lifelong loyalty.

I got in my car and drove down to New South Wales – the trip was less than an hour from my place on the Gold Coast, but I was crossing an invisible line that Rod couldn't.

By the time I reached the address I'd been given, the road beneath me had turned from concrete to gravel to dust. An old dirt road led to a block of land. There was nothing flash about the place; it was just an old shed and a couple of caravans ringed with camp chairs and fireplaces, the little signs of life that let you know this was a home for people who didn't fit in with normal society, for one reason or another.

The shed – a weatherboard and iron number – had a porch. Sitting out there was a big fat bloke. He saw me and waved me over, so I parked the car and walked up the dirt path to say hello. He didn't stand when I approached, but he waved me closer so I could hear him speak.

'I've got Jack Dancer,' he said, barely above a whisper. 'And it ain't good.'

Jack Dancer. Cancer. Right, I thought.

Rod was an intimidating-looking bloke up close, a proper biker, with tattoos snaking up his arms and creeping up his neck from under his shirt. He had chunky silver rings on all his fingers, a big chain around his neck, scars on his knuckles. He was a huge unit by anyone's standard, and I was expecting this big booming voice, but it was so soft that I had to ask him to repeat himself several times and really lean in to hear his story.

He was almost dead, he told me. Not long to go now; he'd done the chemo, the radiation, tried every treatment available, and all of it had only made him sicker. The last two years he'd been sick as a dog. Now he was ready to leave the world.

When you're that sick, you just want to go. You want to get out of the pain, the frustration. You don't want to be a burden on the people who love you. One of Rod's biggest regrets was that if he hadn't done anything and just tried to live with his illness, he would have had a happier final few years.

His nurse, the woman who'd first called me and asked me to come down, came out of the shed to introduce herself. She was lovely; one of those young people you find in the NSW borderlands. A holistic, hippie type who liked living out on the land, away from the hustle of the city, hanging out with the butterflies and the bees. Now she was looking after Rod in his final days.

She fixed us all mugs of tea while we chatted. Once we were settled, Rod got down to brass tacks.

He told me he wanted to be buried with his Harley, and he wanted to hire someone he could trust to make sure that happened. I assured him I could do that. I asked him what else there was.

'So,' he said. 'I'm gay. You might believe that, you might not. I don't really care. I don't give a fuck what you think. All I want to know is what you're willing to do for me when I'm gone.'

He wanted me to interrupt his funeral service and reveal to his friends and associates that he was queer. He was bisexual, and had enjoyed many flings with women over the years, but his preferences had leaned more towards men his whole adult life.

In any case, in his final years he had enjoyed one intense, loving relationship with another man in particular, but had never found a way to tell his brothers in the motorcycle club. This was his main request: that I crash a funeral full of grieving and possibly heavily armed bikers and tell them that the bloke they were putting in the ground had been secretly gay his whole life.

'Yeah mate,' I said. 'No problem, I can do that.'

I told him how much it would cost, and also told him what I wasn't willing to do – he had a long list of demands and grievances he wanted settled. A biker from a rival chapter he wanted sorted out. A chapter member who'd stolen bike parts off him in the past who he wanted me to confront.

I told him no, explaining that I had my own rules. Essentially, I could help him write the final chapter of his own story. If I was going to start rocking up at funerals to sort out shit like that, starting new fights over old grudges, then I was making myself nothing more than a nuisance – I'd become exactly the kind of petty fuckwit that had caused the trouble in the first place.

Rod was taken aback. 'What the fuck do you mean?' he demanded. 'You can't tell me what I can and can't do at my funeral.'

'I fucking can. This is my business. I'm the fucking Coffin Confessor, you're the bloke in the dirt. If you don't like my rules, we don't have to work together.'

I stood up to go and he laughed. This wheezy, broken sort of a chuckle.

He said, 'Okay, nah, nah. That's fine. Sit down.'

This was just part of the negotiations. It was the same dealing with any hard man – there was always a bit of banter at the beginning, a bit of an exchange to test your character. It was about earning the respect you needed to trust each other.

Rod didn't want somebody who was going to be too weak to fulfil his promises, so a little bit of aggro was just a test. He wanted to see if I had the balls to do what he wanted.

It was clear to me that if he weren't at death's door, Rod would have taken things into his own hands. I could tell that this guy had seen some wild shit in his time, and partaken in some proper violence in his prime. Physically, he was pretty much exactly how you'd picture an outlaw biker. At the same time, there was a lot about him I didn't expect; he was worldly, well-educated, well-travelled.

Rod was part of an underworld where the rules were different. Everything there was dictated by unwritten codes. A lot of what we spoke about that day, I didn't have much knowledge of – chapters, brothers, biker codes, all that – but I knew a little bit. I let slip a little bit of information I knew about the Hunters and Rod jumped on it.

'How do you know that?'

'Oh, I met some Hunters in Boggo Road. I did some time there.'

'Bullshit.'

'I did some time with Charlie Main and Coco.'

'Never heard of them. Who are they?'

'Charlie Main was the head Hunter in Boggo. Coco was a Rebels motorcycle rider.'

'You see them much?'

'Nah. Not for years.'

'You know they're dead?' Just as fast as it came, he dropped the pretence he didn't know them. 'Both got killed in crashes ten years ago.'

I shook my head. 'I only knew them from Boggo.'

'Oh yeah? What yard where you in?'

'H Yard. I was just a kid, so I was in the yard for protected prisoners.'

'One Gaol or Two Gaol?'

'Two Gaol.'

'Oh, okay. How were the showers?'

That was a trick question. Two Gaol was the colonial-era part of the prison. It was basically prehistoric. It didn't have proper running water, no more than it had a waiter with a drinks trolley.

Rod was trying a tactic I often use in PI work myself. When I'm questioning someone and I think they might be dodgy, I'll often throw them a curveball, asking about someone or something that doesn't exist. I'll ask about Dave Russo, just a name I've made up, and if the suspect starts banging on about what a top bloke Dave Russo is, I'll know they're full of shit. I'll let them keep going and going, but from then on I know they can't be trusted.

In that scenario, I walk away and refuse to take the job. I guess Rod was doing something similar.

'No,' I told him. 'There was no running water in Two Gaol. It's a shithole.'

'Fuck me! You *were* there!'

'Yeah, I fucking told ya.'

I was impatient now. I was there to help Rod get his affairs in order, not tell him my life story. And there's not much about Boggo Road anyone wants to go out of their way to remember, believe me.

Rod and I had only been speaking for forty-five minutes and the deal was done, right on the spot. He called out to his carer, and she brought out a computer – we did the paperwork right there. Then he went inside, clearly in a great deal of pain, judging from the way he moved. When he came back out, he put $10K right in my hand, cash.

191

I started counting it and his eyes nearly popped out of his head.

'Seriously? Fucking oath – where's the trust?'

'Mate, I don't trust anyone.'

'How am I supposed to trust you?'

'I don't give a fuck if you trust me. I'll either do it or I won't. If I break my word, we're ending up in the same place anyway.' If there's an afterlife, the last thing I need is to get to the gates and have this big, pissed-off ghost biker waiting for me with a steel chain.

'Maybe you're right,' he said. 'Maybe if I'd trusted less I wouldn't have wasted my last time on earth with these useless treatments that only made me sicker.'

'Well, live and learn,' I said.

'Not me. I'm a dead man. No more learning for me.'

'Well, there you go.'

We shook hands and that was that.

I drove back with the money on the passenger seat next to me. Ten thousand dollars, right in my hand.

The second I could, I put it straight into the bank and alerted my accountant. I didn't want to know where Rod's money came from, but I needed a paper trail so I could make sure everything was above board on my end. It would have been easy to pocket it, but it was important to me that this was all ethically and legally above board. A dying man had put his trust in me, so it was important I not fuck anything up.

Now the only thing left to do was carry out my client's wishes without getting murdered by a bunch of grieving bikers dismayed by their friend's secret life.

* * *

Rod passed away not long after our meeting, and while we'd spoken on the phone a couple of times, I never saw him again.

The funeral was actually quite fun. It was a little bit intimidating, sure, but the worst thing that could happen to me was a brawl, and I've always quite enjoyed a brawl.

My main concern, once again, was working out what to wear. I'd gotten more comfortable with that over the Coffin Confessor jobs I'd done since that first one, but what is the dress code at a funeral where most of the mourners are going to be bikers wearing club colours and leather vests?

In the end, I decided my regular uniform would be just fine: a suit and a vest, but with no jacket or tie. It's very respectful attire, and I figured that all the bikers wear vests, so I would sort of blend in a bit, although mine was a beautiful tailor-made suit vest, not leather. Plus, if things went south, it's an easy outfit to swing a punch in.

When I turned up, I did stand out a little from the rest of the mourners. People were a bit confused by me. *Who's this guy?* I kept it vague when they asked who I was, just muttering something about being an old colleague of Rod's. No lie there – his money was safe in my bank account at that very minute.

The service was at the graveside, with chairs set out right beside the grave where the immediate family was supposed to sit. Nobody sat there for now – the seats were empty except for bundles of flowers. There were a couple of girlfriends around, not just one or two, but a whole bunch of women who Rod had been involved with at some point.

I don't know what the story was, why the chairs were empty, but I guess Rod's real family was his brothers in the Hunters.

His whole chapter was there, as well as blokes from other chapters who'd come to pay their respects.

There are all these intricate rules for outlaw motorcycle clubs – the proper and respectful way to wear the coat of arms, how to behave around other chapters. They've got ranks and official titles, like sergeant-at-arms. And there I was, on eggshells, with no idea what any of it fucking meant.

I waited until the proceedings began, then gently made my way to the front of the crowd and introduced myself.

'Excuse me. My name's Bill Edgar and I'm the Coffin Confessor. What you're about to hear comes from your friend and associate, Rod, who has asked me to read this on his behalf.'

I reached into my vest and retrieved the letter Rod had given me.

'Hi, dickheads. I'm dead and you're all still here. Make sure you enjoy what time you have left. Death is a fucking scary adventure. I embraced it – had to really. I don't have much of a choice now, do I?

'Now that I'm gone, I've got something to tell you. As some of you might have known deep down, or suspected: I was bisexual. I was in love with a man, and that man stands amongst you right now.'

I looked up – there was a bit of an uproar. Some of the assembled were shocked, others weren't that happy.

There was no way but forward, so I kept reading.

'I know you're all looking around trying to figure out who he is. You're not going to ever know unless he tells you. But I want him to know I loved him with everything I had. No, it's not David, who right now is probably standing up the back laughing and looking around. You can all stop looking at David.'

'Fuck off, idiot,' said one tough-looking bloke, squaring up to me. 'Who are you to come here and say this shit?'

But then another biker stepped forward and went, 'No, listen. That's Rod. Listen to what he's saying. It sounds exactly like him. He's asked this bloke to come down – that's exactly how he talked.'

The mood changed. If it had been a bit intimidating a second ago, it was suddenly quite comical. The rest of the mourners really got into it, and the response became very positive as I worked through the rest of the letter:

'To those who cared for me, I love you guys. To those that didn't, I'll see you in hell. It's time for me to visit past family and friends, so live well, ride safe, and be true to yourself. That's something I wasn't, but wished I was. Remember me by remembering to live with no regrets.'

And that was that. It felt like Rod had got one last hurrah after his death. His message was important – for him, finally able to come out of the closet, but also for the mourners. We all understood that life doesn't last long at all. Rod was right, that grumpy bastard.

At the end of the service, as per Rod's request, we buried him with his bike – a beautiful 1200cc Harley Davidson Fat Boy. Technically, it's illegal to bury a vehicle in Queensland because there are oils, petrol and chemicals in a bike that can contaminate the groundwater. But I'd made a promise, so into the ground the bike would go.

Prior to the funeral I'd approached the gravediggers and paid them a couple of hundred bucks to make themselves scarce until after the service. One of them, a real grizzled old-timer, told me it wasn't the first time he'd done so.

The Hunters helped me push the bike into the grave, where it would rest on the coffin for the rest of time. Then each of the bikers took turns shovelling dirt onto the grave, everyone participating. It happened so fast that by the time the gravediggers did turn up, the work was done. Rod and his bike were interred together. After that, I was gone.

* * *

A week later, Rod's lover called me. He said he tracked me down through my other business, Freedom from Debt Collectors, and told me he wanted to thank me for not outing him. He thought the service was beautiful, funny and touching.

'When my time comes, I'll be doing the same thing,' he said.

We spoke for a little while, and he became very emotional. It was hard for him to lose Rod and he still couldn't believe that they'd spent their years together keeping their love a secret from those closest to them.

'I'm doing fine, I really am,' he said. 'But at the same time, it's 2018. Can you believe we still have to live in fear?'

He told me that one day he'd wanted to come out and live openly with Rod, but they'd never found a way. He was really sad that they'd never been able to be together in public. The way he told it, Rod had lived life the way he rode, utterly without fear, never backing down from anything – except this.

While this poor guy cried on the phone to me, he was really confronted by this fact. But he was glad that, at least after he was gone, Rod was able to share this side of himself with the world.

After I hung up, I sat there thinking for a good while. What a fucking shame. It was like that movie, *Brokeback Mountain*. Only Brokeback Biker, I guess. Brokeback Gold Coast. Sad for Rod, of course, and his lover, but sad as well for all the other dudes still living in the closet because they are scared of how those around them might react.

I've known many men like that, socially or in my PI work. Gay men who keep it on the down low forever, even getting married to hide it. That starts a whole cycle of betrayal, not just lying to the women they marry but also to themselves.

Everyone has their secrets. Most people are buried with them. Looking back, I'm glad Rod got to share this one, and was buried with the best wishes of his brothers in the gang, and one beautiful fucking motorcycle.

18

Run for your life

Solitary isolation is not a good time. They call it 'the hole' for a reason.

It's a unique kind of psychological torture to be locked in a tiny room with nothing to do, nobody to talk to, no form of human interaction. Human beings are social animals – we're not designed to live that way. The most tough-minded people might be fine for a few days, maybe a week at most, but then even they would start to crack.

It's not good to be alone with your thoughts for that long. Especially when you've got as many difficult things to think about as I did.

During my time in isolation, I was approached by a guard of high authority named Patty O'Connor. He was a prison institution in himself – a big, tough-as-nails screw with a strong Irish accent. He pulled up a chair alongside the cage I was in and sat down. Across his knees he held a piece of paper, neatly folded.

'I knew your father, Billy,' he told me. 'I knew him well. Real well.'

He handed me the piece of paper and I unfolded it. I saw a face resembling mine staring up at me from a black-and-white photo. That was the first time I'd ever seen a picture of my dad.

I'd known my dad had been to prison, but I didn't know he'd been to Boggo Road. At that point, I didn't really know anything about him. All I knew was that he came and went a bit when I was a baby. He left for the last time when I was about three years old.

My mum had always told me he was dead. She hated him, and hated me because I had his name. As I'd grown up, and started to look more like him, she began to hate me more and more. So it was never a particularly nice experience talking to Mum about Dad, and I soon learned to forget all about it.

Looking at that photo, I realised I *had* met him, once, long ago. At primary school one day a guy turned up and hung around just outside the schoolyard gate, watching me play. That afternoon, when I was walking home, he called me over. He knelt down and had a good look at my face, then gave me a pat on the head.

'You be a good boy for your mum,' he said, then walked away.

That was my dad. He must have been about to go to prison and didn't think he'd be seeing me again.

Chances are I would have gone my whole life without ever knowing what he looked like if Patty O'Connor hadn't brought me that photo.

We sat there a while and Patty told me all about my old man. He'd been a famous hard man, starting as a bouncer for the night-clubs of Kings Cross and making his name as a boxer. He was known as 'the Irishman' and was a famous southpaw – the right hand out the front for quick punches, the left held back as the big hitter.

From there, he became known as a standover man for the trade unions, then for various organised crime operations across Australia, and finally a hitman. Apparently, he'd been done on extortion and a serious assault charge after an incident at the Gold Coast Beer Garden, which finally brought him to Boggo Road.

There, he was one of the most feared men in the place. Patty told me that he'd run his side of the prison, kept the Irish faction in line, made sure everything was done fairly and nobody spoke out of turn. The weak were protected and the really nasty pieces of work were taken care of.

The way Patty told it, he was a prison legend.

'That's your old man's cell, right over there – 2202.' He pointed across the hallway to another cage identical to the one I was locked in.

'He was a real gentleman, your father. He kept the law around here,' he said. 'Do me a favour, Billy?'

'What's that?'

'Don't end up like him.'

He got up and walked off, leaving me with the photo.

I was ashamed. I know they say the apple doesn't fall far from the tree, but I was hoping that it would roll a little further than the next fucking prison cell. How much further could I hope for my son to get in life if this was the sort of example I was setting?

* * *

Lara had been coming to visit me throughout my time at Boggo Road, and usually she'd bring our son. The next time I saw her, I told her never to bring him again. I didn't want him anywhere near the place.

Three generations of Edgar men under the one prison roof. I felt so guilty. Just absolutely fucked. It's indescribable how hard the separation from my son was for me. He was eight weeks old when I went to jail. I missed the first two years of his life because I'd fucked up. Lara was left to raise him more or less on her own.

It's terrible, what I put her through. Why she's still with me today, I'll never know. Every time she came to visit, the baby had grown so much. It was so fucking hard to see what I'd done to her.

But you know what? It inspired me to become a better person, to do something with my life, to become somebody she could be proud of.

I never would have made it without her. She taught me to take all my negative feelings – the resentment, the hurt, the despair, the rage – and turn them into something positive. They became the fuel for me to keep doing the work it took to keep it together until I got out of jail. If things weren't going well, she wouldn't let me give up.

'Bill, if you give up on yourself, you give up on us,' she told me when she came to visit. 'If things aren't going well, just dust yourself off and get the fuck up.'

And so I never gave up – because of her. She was beautiful. Just an incredible woman, to stand by me through my time in prison. She taught me how to shrug things off and keep moving. I had to.

Even walking out of the visiting room, the prison guards would have a go, ribbing me as they walked me back to my cell, marching on either side of me.

'Your missus is stuck in Brisbane now. Can't get home on the train this late at night,' one guard said. 'I might look after her, show her a good time.'

Then the other one chimed in. 'The boy, too. Take him to McDonald's, buy him a cheeseburger, give the mum a bit of cock.'

I'd be ropable, but I always had Lara's advice still ringing in my ears. I'd just laugh it off and walk away.

It worked, too. Little by little, that became my coping strategy. It was how I planned to stay out of trouble for the rest of my sentence.

* * *

But it's not that easy to stay out of trouble in a place like Boggo Road. It's almost impossible to avoid conflict – if someone knows you're not looking for a fight, they're going to pick a fight with you. The lifers would bash you to rape you, to steal your dinner, to steal a cigarette, or just because they were bored.

Because of that, it was pretty standard for some guys to go to prison for a relatively minor crime, end up in a violent altercation while defending themselves, and find themselves with months or years stacked on their sentence. Guys like Simon.

I was in the prison yard one day, doing the usual – pacing, little oval laps of the yard, making the most of the small amount of fresh air and exercise I was granted – when a new bloke came in. As usual, me and every other bloke on that yard quietly sized him up.

He looked like a typical enough bloke. Not all that threatening, but all the same he didn't look weak either. He, too, started to pace up and down. He caught my eye, said hello, and we got to talking.

For the next forty minutes, until we were called back to our cells, Simon told me his whole life story. He wasn't even in for a proper crime, he was just down on his luck. He'd been arrested for not paying parking and speeding fines, and was given the option of serving three months in lieu of paying his debt. Three months in prison seemed like the best option to him – he had no job, but he did have a wife and kids in government housing, which they stood to lose because they were too far behind in rent.

At this point, I was missing my own family badly, and so I felt sorry for the poor guy. I decided to take Simon under my wing. I spent some time letting him know where to sit, who to avoid.

More importantly, I gave him a piece of information that I thought he'd find very useful. As it happened, I'd known some blokes who'd come in with a three-month sentence but stayed only a fortnight, having been released on parole due to prison overcrowding. I thought this news would comfort Simon, and sure enough, it cheered him right up.

Later that day, Simon's name was called out, and he was taken out of his cell and allocated to another wing, where he would complete his three-month sentence.

Five months later, I saw Simon again. He was harder now. He had that look in his eye that you see in guys who have done really hard time. I found out he'd stabbed another inmate, and then been caught with drugs; he had been sentenced to another six years.

One day, years later – on the outside – I opened the newspaper and read that Simon had again been sentenced to six years for violent crime. I thought of the man I'd met on the yard who'd failed to pay a parking ticket, and the family he might never see again. A shiver ran up my spine.

* * *

During my time in prison, I learned there was no such thing as a typical criminal. I met people of all races, creeds and nationalities. There were the good, the bad and the ugly. Some were everyday people – plumbers, electricians, builders, truck drivers – who'd fallen victim to a terrible combination of bad decisions and bad luck. Not to mention the few that had done nothing other than being in the wrong place at the wrong time.

Others were just plain evil. So cruel they would haunt your nightmares.

But in my experience, whatever their background, most prisoners were just doing their time without looking for any conflict or hassle. Jail introduced me to people that had heart, courage and self-worth. There were those who would never commit another crime for as long as they lived, either because they were truly sorry for their crimes or because they had been scared straight by prison.

Discovering the hard way that there is always someone bigger, stronger, faster and smarter than you quickly teaches you that silence is golden. Prison can make or break you, and sometimes it has the ability to do both in a day.

But that's about all it teaches you. The judicial system is deeply flawed in this country – incarceration is a primitive solution to complicated social problems. And yet what should be the last resort is often the first.

I can't say I can recommend prison as a way to rehabilitate someone whose life has gone off the rails. It was Lara who saved me; her love and my son. If it weren't for them, I would have gone on running messages and bashing people up and getting caught in endless cycles of revenge, bloodshed and bullshit.

Some people who would otherwise live perfectly good lives make one mistake too many and end up spending their whole fucking lives behind bars. Some people don't even make it that far.

* * *

One month before I was due to be released, I was moved from high-security Boggo Road to a prison farm called Woodford. It was a low-security facility that relied on the honour system. The cells were often left open, and you could come and go from them as you pleased, provided you behaved yourself and were respectful to the guards and the other prisoners.

You had the opportunity to work the fields in fresh air and sunshine, which was a kind of miracle after all that time spent in a cell. Even the other prisoners were easier to live with – for the most part, you were only sent to the farm if you weren't deemed a risk to yourself or others. It was full of veteran prisoners who'd had all the violence beaten out of them years ago or young men deemed good prospects for rehabilitation.

One of these young blokes, he must have been about seventeen, entered the yard at Woodford. He was new and clearly frightened, and he thought he'd make an impression by lashing out at anyone who looked at him sideways. No doubt he'd been given the old wisdom about asserting dominance from day one in order to avoid becoming a victim. Unfortunately, he'd had a target on his back even before he'd set foot through the gates of Woodford.

Arriving with him was another prisoner. I knew him already by reputation – he was known through the prison system as a proper psychopath. Although he was only twenty, he'd already spent most of his life behind bars. He was as tough and mean as any man I'd encountered.

The word was he was doing a double life sentence for murdering his siblings. Apparently, he'd killed them with his bare hands, then brought his parents in to show them his handiwork, asking them if they were happy that it was just the three of them now.

When I first heard that story, I recall thinking that was really fucked up, even for a place filled to the brim with fucked-up stories.

Now Psycho was in the prison yard. Who knows how the fuck he'd got himself sent to Woodford. He watched this new young bloke – the kid was doing what all new prisoners do, pacing up and down, trying to look intimidating, contemplating his situation and how he was going to handle life behind bars.

Psycho wandered over to him and started walking beside him, from the gates at one end of the yard to the amenities block at the other, back and forth, back and forth. The two men seemed to be chatting, just engaging in small talk, when suddenly, without warning and in mid-sentence, Psycho grabbed the young bloke in a headlock and dragged him into the toilets. For a moment you could hear him screaming for help, then a sickening thud that echoed all the way across the yard. The kid went quiet.

I stood up and was making my way to the toilets when somebody grabbed my arm and spun me around to face him. It was a bloke I knew called Ian, a real grizzled old-timer – heavily built, heavily tattooed, eyes like concrete.

I'd never spoken much to Ian, but Ian kept to himself and didn't speak much to anyone. I was surprised that he'd been the one to stop me. For a moment we stood face to face, staring. He shook his head, just a little, to tell me not to intervene.

I was angry. I told Ian to fuck off and let me help, but he didn't release his vice-like grip.

'You've got less than a month,' he said in a very quiet voice. 'If you don't want to be here for the rest of your life, go back to your cell, Billy.'

With that, he let go of my arm. I knew that he was right.

I went back to my cell and spent the rest of the day brooding about what I should have done.

That evening I heard the new kid being escorted to his cell, which was directly opposite mine. Around 9.30 that night, I heard a scream from the cell, followed by a choking noise and a series of loud bangs, which became weaker and weaker until they stopped. I jumped to my feet and started hammering on my cell door, yelling for the guards.

For ages there was no response, then a solitary guard came walking down the hall. Suddenly the alarm was ringing and prison officers came running from all directions. The kid's cell door swung open and I saw them cut the body down. He'd fashioned a noose from his sheets and hanged himself.

I watched as they worked on him, one officer pounding on his chest, another blowing air into his mouth. This went on for several minutes, until both guards looked up and at each other, one shaking his head.

They placed a blanket over the body and about fifteen minutes later they carried him out on a stretcher. The whole prison watched the guards carry out the body of the poor kid; we'd all stood by earlier in the day as he'd been violated in the prison toilets.

I turned away, sick to my stomach. Tears started rolling down my face, and then I couldn't stop weeping. That was the first time I'd cried in prison. I didn't cry when I was bashed by the screws, or dragged to solitary, or kept away from my family. But I cried for that young man, having turned away from helping him.

* * *

The next morning at breakfast, the mess hall was subdued. We all sat in silence, still reflecting on what had taken place. Word reached us that the young bloke had left a note, saying he couldn't live with himself after being raped. I was sitting there, digesting this news, ignoring my breakfast, when his rapist, Psycho, walked into the dining hall.

'Weak faggots,' he announced. 'The world is full of them.'

He stared down everyone in the room, then sat down to eat as calmly as if he were having a nice breakfast in a hotel restaurant.

Rage overcame me. I wanted nothing more than to walk up to him and inflict as much pain on him as I could before the guards brought me down. My fork was gripped in my fist, and I realised my hand was shaking, imagining going to work on Psycho with it.

It would be easy to take out an eye or two before he could react. Then, from across the room, Ian caught my eye. He gave me another little shake of the head. No.

I calmed down, left breakfast and went to my cell. I sure didn't feel good about it though.

That cycle of violence is inescapable for some. A couple of weeks after that, there was some commotion in the yard and I saw that Ian had knocked down Psycho and was dragging him into the toilet block. He looked up and saw me watching, and a little smile flickered over his face.

A prison guard had seen what was going on, and he made a show of discreetly looking away. The guard clocked that I had seen him do it, and he smiled. 'Karma,' he said. 'It's a wonderful thing.'

* * *

I needed to get out of that shithole. That last stretch until my release seemed to drag endlessly. I spent most of my time either in the gym or in the prison library, although 'library' was a generous description. It was in terrible shape – all the books were classics like *Moby Dick* and *The Great Gatsby*, shit like that. Half the pages were missing and the covers were torn off. Even the Bibles had pages missing. If you ran out of rolling papers, book pages were ideal for rolling cigarettes.

Still, the books were enough for me to practise reading and, slowly, slowly, I taught myself a way to compensate for my dyslexia.

Those last weeks were spent reading – reading and counting down the days, then the minutes. Then one Sunday, a few days before I was due for release, a guard came to the yard yelling my name.

'Pack your bags, Billy-boy!' he yelled. 'You're going home early.'

I couldn't believe my good luck. It was unheard of for a prisoner to be released on a Sunday. Most of the other prisoners were very happy for me, although a few were more cynical, telling me they would see me again before the month's end.

As I packed my gear and was getting ready to leave the prison, Ian came over to me.

'Life is real short, Bill,' he said. He held out his hand and I shook it. 'Make it what you want, but don't make it back inside.'

It was another four hours before I was released, as I had to be transported back to Boggo Road in Brisbane for processing. Once I got there, I learned the reason for my early release, and it wasn't good news. Lara's mother had died unexpectedly. I was being released on compassionate grounds to be able to be with her as she mourned.

From processing, I was escorted to the large iron gates that I'd first entered. But before I got there, a prisoner threw a pair of shoes at me.

'These don't fit me right!' he yelled. 'They're a size eleven.'

I looked at the shoes and realised they were mine; they were the ones I'd been robbed of on my first day. I looked at the prisoner and gave him a nod, taking off my prison shoes and putting my own shoes on.

My heart was hammering in my chest, my mouth was dry, my palms were slick with sweat. I was sure something or someone was going to stop me from leaving.

I noticed officer Patty O'Connor walking towards me, but he'd only come to see me off. 'Don't be coming back this way now, will you, Billy?'

Then the prison gates began to creak open, revealing the most beautiful sight for a prisoner: daylight.

It might be impossible for someone who hasn't been incarcerated to understand what it feels like to have the free sun on your face again. Daylight was a luxury in prison – a commodity that was doled out to us with the meagre amount of time we were given for exercise. I'd stand in the yard and stare up at a little square of blue sky beyond the prison walls and crave freedom. Now here it was, the bright Brisbane sun spilling through the gates to welcome me back to the world.

Patty escorted me through the large iron gates. Once I was on the other side, I bent down and untied my shoelaces, taking my shoes off for the second time in twenty minutes. I put them neatly on the ground beside my feet and started to walk away from the prison wearing only my socks.

'What the fuck are you doing, Billy?' Patty yelled out.

'Those shoes brought me in there,' I yelled over my shoulder without turning. 'They're not bringing me back.'

To this day, I can still hear Patty's laughter ringing in my ears.

19

Regrets, I've had a few

Think about freedom. If you had to choose an image, a symbol to represent 'freedom', what would it be? A surfboard on a deserted reef break? A motorcycle tearing down a highway? What about a boat? There's not much in the world that says 'I'm free' like owning a boat.

Of course it's more complicated than that. Freedom is a double-edged blade. It can make or break a life, depending on what you do with it.

Generally, when someone lives on a boat, it means one of two things. One reason is that your life is great and you've worked hard, invested well and spent your hard-earned on a leisure craft. You use it to enjoy a happy retirement surrounded by friends and family, making the most of your twilight years.

The other reason is you've fucked your life up completely.

There's a certain kind of old man that lives on a boat purely because he's made such a mess of his life that there's nothing to keep him on dry land anymore.

Jackson was in that camp.

Prior to being admitted to hospital, he had spent his days on a run-down, 38-foot sloop yacht, moored on a lake by a town in rural Queensland. He was the sort of bloke who had little in his life but secrets; he was the hermit type, and probably had a lot to get away from.

I believe I've rarely met a man who had so many regrets. He hated the town, hated the townsfolk, hated strangers, hated me and, more than anything, hated himself. A really bitter old man who just radiated loathing. Whenever I meet somebody, I know straight away if they are bad news, and that first impression is rarely wrong. If I couldn't size someone up pretty quickly, I wouldn't have lasted long on the streets as a kid.

Some people look for the good in everyone, believing that even the worst people have some redeeming feature. I'm the opposite – my ears are pricked for the first sign of something bad about someone, and once I sense it that's all I can focus on.

Jackson wanted me to make contact with his daughter, who he was estranged from. I don't know what he'd done to bring that about, but whatever it was, it wasn't good. She hated his guts. She wanted nothing to do with him and wouldn't speak to him. He'd let her know he was dying and she didn't give a shit.

Where all this animosity came from, Jackson never came out and told me, but I suspect he was your garden-variety shitty, abusive dad. The world is full of them.

I can't say it was good to meet with the man, or that I came away feeling particularly sympathetic to his plight. But his request seemed harmless enough: he wanted his estate to go to his daughter, and he wanted me to take it to her.

All he had in the world was this boat, and whatever dismal possessions he had inside it. It can't have been worth all that much, but he wanted her to have it, and that seemed fair to me.

He handed me an envelope. On the outside was his daughter's name, Mel, and inside was the deed to the boat and his will. I took his payment, shook his hand and left.

* * *

Jackson died not long after our meeting, and I set out to carry out his final wish.

Mel's number and email address were easy to find, along with her residence and place of work. As a first step, I tried to contact her through phone and email, but the only response I got from her was a text: 'Leave me alone.'

I would have been happy to do so, but I had given my word at Jackson's deathbed, and nothing was going to stop me from seeing that through.

Mel had settled down in a small tourist town in northern Queensland. I booked a room in a cheap, anonymous motel, and made the twenty-hour drive up there, collapsing into bed on arrival.

The rising sun woke me, together with the soundtrack of a small tourist town – seagulls and surf. I had Mel's home address, but I didn't want to bother her at home if it could be avoided. I took a chance and drove to the cafe where she worked.

When I got there, the breakfast rush was just finishing. It was a lovely little cafe – a little bit retro, with eighties decor and chess-board flooring. I'd spent countless hours in cafes like that as a kid, using them as a place to get off the streets, until they realised I wasn't paying and kicked me out.

Five staff were on, four women and one man. I took a seat and waited for someone to come over and take my coffee order, a latte, extra hot. It was impossible to work out from physical appearance if any of these women were Jackson's daughter – I recognised nothing of the gnarled old man I'd met in any of these young women. None of the staff wore name badges, just a branded shirt with the name of the cafe.

When the bloke brought over my coffee, I figured he had the information I needed.

'Mel not working today, mate?' I asked him.

He glanced up. 'Yeah, she's on the coffee machine,' he said. 'Maybe you didn't recognise her under that stupid hat.'

I glanced over at the coffee machine, and the woman working it. I couldn't really make out her face under a garish hot-pink cap she was wearing.

'Oh yeah, there she is.' I smiled at the guy. 'You're right, that is a stupid hat. Thanks for the coffee.'

I observed Mel for a few minutes while drinking my coffee. It was important to get this right, as I would only get one shot at it. She was young, blonde, friendly with the people she interacted with, but with the sort of face where I could tell at a glance that she'd struggled. Two deep lines that ran up from her jaw testified to a great deal of anguish and hard work in her short life.

Her accent was thick and broadly Queensland, a bit rough, but she was unfailingly polite and well-spoken with customers. She couldn't have been more different from that grumpy bastard on the boat, really.

To make sure of her identity, I switched my phone to private and called her once there were no customers waiting and she had opportunity to answer. She reached into her pocket, looked at her phone, saw the private number and then put it back in her pocket. Only then was I sure I had the right woman.

I got up with my coffee cup and approached the counter.

'Excuse me,' I said.

'Yes?' she said, glancing down at the coffee in my hand. 'Is there something wrong with your coffee?'

'The coffee is great, thank you,' I said. I placed the envelope on the counter, then placed the coffee cup on top of it. 'Have a wonderful day.'

My job was done; I walked away without looking back. Whether what was in the envelope made Mel happy, or sad, or angry – if she even opened it at all or threw it in the bin – that was none of my business. I'd carried out Jackson's final wish and now he could rest in peace.

I was eager to get home. I missed my family, and it was going to be a long drive back to them. I didn't want to waste any time. I hate being away from them for long.

20

Real life

When I walked out of prison, I knew I was never walking back in. I went straight back to the Gold Coast, where Lara was staying with my sister. When I got there she was asleep on the couch, so I lay down next to her and held her. She was startled to see me – happy, of course, but just absolutely devastated by the loss of her mum.

But finally Lara was by my side, as she had been in spirit all through my incarceration. She'd been my rock and my inspiration, but we were about to go through new challenges neither of us was prepared for.

During my time in lock-up, she and our son had lived with her parents, but we couldn't do that in the future. We were trying our hardest to make a home. We moved into a caravan in a caravan park, but we couldn't even afford the rent on that, so we moved into a tent.

Work was scarce on the Gold Coast. There just weren't many employers chomping at the bit to hire a teenager, with no education and no experience, who'd just gotten out of prison. And without reading or writing skills, or even identity papers, I didn't have the capacity to get my car licence, which put me out of the running for most labour contract jobs.

Lara and I decided it was best to move on and start fresh. We loaded up her car, a white Datsun 180B with a black vinyl roof, and hit the road. We had decided to head to a town called Airlie Beach, which is halfway between Brisbane and Cairns. The car was too worn-out to get us much further than that anyway.

We were too broke to find accommodation other than a tent in the local caravan park. It was one step above being homeless, but even that arrangement was almost unsustainable. Week to week, we could barely scrape together the cash to pay for the dirt our tent was pitched on.

It was a really hard time. They say marriage has its ups and downs, but it was definitely more downs than ups back then.

We tried our hardest to make it work, scraping by on welfare money. After paying the rent, we could afford to buy bread, milk and nothing else. Some weeks we didn't even have enough for that.

I remember the days in the lead-up to our first Christmas in Airlie Beach. One morning we were in the local supermarket and realised that we did not have enough money for basic groceries. We had to choose between food and nappies for our son. I was standing there holding a loaf of bread in one hand and a bag of nappies in the other, trying to decide which we needed more urgently. It was hard not to notice the full trolleys passing us by, each filled to overflowing with Christmas hams, cakes, puddings, fruit and vegetables.

Our son had picked up a chocolate bar and was running up and down the confectionary aisle. Then a Christmas jingle he liked came on over the radio and he stopped to dance to it.

It was a sight that brought a smile to my face, but when I turned to Lara, she was in tears. She was breaking down before my eyes. She dropped to her knees, covering her mouth with her hand to hold back the sobs.

I picked her up and tried to comfort her, but there was no consoling her – she was physically and emotionally exhausted. I'd just gotten out of prison, her mother had died, and we were destitute. We had no money, not even enough for a plastic toy for our son's Christmas present. Not even for the chocolate bar he was holding.

Our son was just two years old, but he knew when things weren't right. The moment he saw the state his mother was in, he threw the chocolate bar to the ground. He walked up to us and Lara held him tight. He tried to wipe away his mother's tears, but the more he tried the more they flowed.

After a short while we all composed ourselves, paid for our meagre groceries, and headed back to our tent.

I didn't exactly feel great about myself right then, but I didn't know what the fuck I was going to do. All I knew was that I loved my wife and kid, and I was going to find a way to look after them. I promised them that we would never go hungry or without again. I promised them that things were going to change. And they did.

I went into every shop in that town, asking for work, but found nothing at all.

It wasn't until I was returning to the caravan park that my luck finally changed. There was a road crew working on a partially paved road out the front, and the workmen were sitting under a tree, seeking shade in the midday heat.

I approached and asked if there was any work available.

One bloke stood up. He was tall, solidly built and very tanned from working in the hot sun all day, every day.

'Do you know how to use a shovel?' he said.

'Of course.'

'Well, there's one over there.' He pointed to a large heap of gravel. 'Get shovelling.'

Apparently, the bobcat they were using to pave the road had broken down, but the gravel needed to be moved before the next load arrived, which would be in about three hours.

With my t-shirt wrapped around my head, I began to shovel. I didn't stop until nightfall.

When the boss man came over to see me, he gave the work I'd done a glancing once-over, then grunted. He didn't say 'good job' or even ask my name. He just said, 'See you at six.'

The next morning, I was there at six, and the day after that, and the day after that.

On the fourth day, the boss handed me an envelope full of cash.

'Thought you'd have run away by now,' he said.

'Why's that?'

'Most blokes only work a day or two. Gets too hot and hard for them out here.'

'No, not me. I've got a family that deserves a better life. If this is what it takes, then so be it.'

He squinted at me. 'Your name's Bill, right?'

'Yep.'

'I'm Mike. But don't think we're friends.'

'Don't need a friend, Mike. Just a job.'

Mike laughed at that and walked away. I continued to shovel, but Mike turned back and said, 'That's enough for today, Billy. Good job. See you Monday.'

So I had a job. Inside the envelope was $600. Mike had paid me for a full week of work, even though I'd only done four days. I'd never encountered that sort of generosity before. It was unbelievable.

I packed away the tools and headed back to the caravan park. Lara and our son were playing in the pool, and I jumped in, splashing about like a little kid. We were ecstatic.

After our swim, we went out to look for presents for our son, and to the chicken shop for a much-needed feed of chicken and chips. Mate, that's the best fucking Christmas lunch I've ever had.

I knew if I could work for the next two weeks, I could earn enough to rent a small unit for the three of us, and that's exactly what I did. I worked four or five days a week, shovelling stones and gravel, and before too long we were able to move from the unit to a nice little house.

Each day, as I left for work, I stopped in at the local store to buy an apple. And on the way home I'd come through again to buy a treat for Lara and our son. Over time I became friends with the shop's owner, Johnno. Each morning he would throw me an apple, then have a coffee brewing for me on the way home.

One day, breaking the routine, Johnno invited me for a hot cup of coffee in the morning. I'd just had coffee at home, but to be polite I accepted it, figuring I would just drink it as quick as I could. But he surprised me with an offer: he needed some help around the store, and would pay me a week's wage to work three days a week.

I was overjoyed – now I was working indoors, in air-conditioning, with all the fresh food I could handle. What more could I want?

* * *

I had been working for Johnno for about twelve months when he decided to close up shop. He wanted to spend more time on his land, with his family.

Once upon a time I might have seen this as a setback, but by then I knew I had enough experience to run my own shop. A week after Johnno closed, I opened up my own place. Everything was bought on credit – the food, the shelving, even the first month's rent. But after that, I was able to pay back the creditors while purchasing stock that would make the store more competitive with the major stores.

It was around then that Lara found out she was pregnant again. We were over the moon, and I asked her to marry me. Full disclosure – this wasn't the first time, but she'd always turned me down before. She's since told me that she first needed me to figure out who I was. That she didn't think I was ready to get married.

That time, after everything we'd been through, I guess she thought I was ready. She said yes.

We had a small ceremony, down at the marina on Lara's dad's boat. It was only seven people in total, but the day was still a total disaster. Oh, it was terrible.

The morning of the wedding I was really nervous, and my mate was trying to calm me down. He told me to have a little marijuana, that it would get rid of the nerves.

I don't know why I did it; I didn't even like marijuana.

I don't remember a single thing from that day, except the perfectly clear image of Lara in her dress. The rest is a write-off. I was a mess.

Lara was really hurt by the whole thing, but in the scheme of things, it wasn't the dumbest thing I'd ever done.

* * *

Everything was going well, and life was good. We had a beautiful little house, which Lara had made a home, and we had friends and a business of our own. Even better, Lara was pregnant with our second child.

Then, without warning, Airlie Beach became a ghost town.

It happened virtually overnight. The nation's airlines went on strike, which meant no one could fly in or out, and that was the start of the demise.

All around us, businesses were closing and people were moving away in droves. The tradesmen with families, who had been building the resorts on nearby Hamilton Island, had to pack up and move, looking for work in other parts of the state.

We held on for as long as we could but eventually, like most people in town, we were forced to close and leave our beautiful life in Airlie Beach.

It was time for another change, and we decided on a move to South Australia.

There was nothing stopping us from doing what we wanted, so on our way there we stopped in Sydney, to visit Lara's sister but also so Lara could give birth to our daughter. We basically just stopped by the hospital long enough to have a kid, then got back on the road.

It was insane, now that I think about it. What were we thinking? What was *I* thinking? We left for South Australia a day or two after Lara gave birth, and I believe these circumstances contributed to her post-natal depression, which plagued her for some years after this. I'd fucked up yet again.

* * *

Arriving in South Australia, we fell in love with the Barossa Valley. I found a fruit shop close to Adelaide whose owner was looking for an operator; I applied for the job over the phone and, on attending the interview the next day, I got the job right away.

We moved into a nice house with a row of fruit trees in the backyard. I worked almost every day, while Lara looked after our children. But my hours at the shop meant I was never home, and the stress of not knowing anyone or having family close by only worsened Lara's depression.

After six months, we returned to the Gold Coast.

* * *

My daughter had just turned two, and it had been a struggle the whole way. Lara had been battling post-natal depression for those two years, and I'd been in and out of work through it all.

I'd done every job I could find, but there were some weeks when I just couldn't find any. No matter how hard I tried, I just couldn't provide for my family.

And then, one day, I found work that took me away from my family for three weeks. When I came home, I found a note. Lara had left me.

It was a devastating blow. She hadn't told me she was leaving, and I hadn't seen it coming at all. She'd moved to Cairns to live with her sister.

I just sat there in the lounge room of our rental, holding this note, which I felt was proof I'd failed my family yet again.

'Fuck, what have I done?' I said to myself. 'I've lost my wife and kids.'

It was a real punch to the gut, the worst feeling. I couldn't believe this was what my life had come to.

* * *

For some reason, after Lara left, more work started coming in – it was fucking pathetic timing. Finally I could have provided for my wife and kids, but they were gone.

Lara contacted me a couple of times, telling me that she was okay, that the kids were fine, but I just hung up the phone. I didn't ever want to hear from her again.

I had a lot of hate, for her and for myself. The guilt was overwhelming. I just shut down completely. I worked around the clock – hard labour in the day, nightclub bouncer at night. All I could manage to do was go to work, then come back home and stare at the phone. It rang all the time, but I wouldn't answer it. As hard as it was to be away from my kids, to not be talking to them every day, I refused to do so.

Three months passed that way. And then, one day, I just picked up the phone. It was my son, five years old by now.

'Daddy? Don't hang up,' he said.

I'll never forget it. I couldn't believe it. For a while I just sat with the phone to my ear, listening to him talk; he'd been going to school in Cairns, he missed me so much, Mummy was very sad without me.

'When are you going to come and see us?' he said.

I didn't respond. I couldn't! I wasn't able to get any words out of my throat. I heard him say, 'Mum, he's not talking to me.'

That's when I cracked.

'Mate, mate. I'm right here. I heard what you said.'

He told me he loved me and I told him the same, and that I missed him and his sister very much.

Then he passed the phone to his mum.

I heard him running away from the phone to go play with his sister, and I remember thinking, *Oh, it's nice that he doesn't hate me.*

Then Lara was on the phone. She'd gotten a place with her sister and a job in Cairns. She was sorting herself out. Things were okay.

'But there's something I'm missing,' she said. 'It's you.'

'I can't do it,' I told her. 'I can't go up there and be a failure as well. I just can't do it. You've moved on. I've got to accept that.'

'Bill,' she said. 'Don't be an idiot. It's been three months. You don't move on from your husband in three months.'

It took some time, but she convinced me. Convinced me that I needed to get away from the Gold Coast, that Cairns was a new start, a new chance at a new life.

I realised that we had to give it a crack, and work really hard at putting our family back together.

Pretty much straight after I hung up the phone, I was on the road. Across the street from the caravan park I was living in was an auto wrecker's yard. Every day I'd pass it and see this old Valiant, sitting up on a ramp.

When I walked in, there were six days' rego left on the plate. The price was written in marker on the window: $580. I had $500 to my name.

'Would you take $500 cash?' I asked the wrecker.

'No worries,' he said.

'Do you reckon it'll make it to Cairns?'

'I reckon it'll make it three-quarters of the way.' He laughed. 'Then you can hitch from there.'

'That'll do me.' We shook on it.

It was the best car I ever had. Brilliant. It got me all the way to Lara's front door before giving up. A fucking miracle.

From there, I walked to her office. When Lara saw me, she dropped everything and ran up to me. We had a bit of a cuddle, then we left and went to pick up the kids. They couldn't stop crying, but to be fair, neither could I.

We got a place in a small mobile home in a caravan park and stayed there together for a couple of weeks until we found a nice house. We moved in, and started rebuilding from there.

* * *

Before I'd left the Gold Coast, I had gone around saying goodbye to everyone I'd been working with. A couple of the boys I'd bounced nightclubs with told me there was plenty of security work in Cairns, and that I should try out for door jobs at some of the clubs up there.

There was a place called Tropos, housed in an old colonial hotel, that was a notorious backpacker spot. The boys were sure I could find work there. But one of the old-timers encouraged me to aim higher.

'If you're really good at what you do, Bill – and you're pretty good – you should go to the Playpen International. It's the best club in Queensland.'

So I had made that my goal. All the way to Cairns, I kept thinking about this place called Playpen International. I had made up my mind to work there. No matter what, I was going to get that job, work hard, work my way up, and really make something out of it.

By the time I reached the Cairns city limits, I had all these aspirations, a plan to be the manager at that nightclub in a couple of years. I knew fuck-all about managing a nightclub, but I'd gotten this idea into my head, and once I had momentum it was hard to discourage me from doing anything I'd set my mind to.

That first day, after meeting up with Lara, I went straight to the Playpen. When I got there, I saw a guy up a ladder, changing light globes on the sign out the front. There was a bouncer down below, holding the ladder – this big unit, with a nametag that read 'Jeffery 141'. I went up to talk to him.

'Hey, mate. Jeffery, is it? I'm new in town and looking for work.'

'No work here.'

'Are you the boss, manager or owner?'

'No. I'm the doorman.'

I didn't like hearing that. This prick wasn't being very helpful, and he had my job.

I called up at the bloke at the top of the ladder. 'What about you, mate? Know of any work here?'

'Who's asking?' he called back.

'Me! My name's Bill, I'm just up from the Gold Coast. Who are you?'

'I'm the owner, Brett.'

'You're the owner?' I laughed. He was so high up on the ladder, I figured he must have been the janitor. 'This guy's down here holding the ladder while you're risking your neck up there? Something's gone fucking wrong here, Brett. I heard this is the best club in Cairns, but I've obviously come to the wrong place.'

'What do you mean?'

'Well, put it this way, Brett. If I walk up to Jeffery here and knock him out, then would you give me a job?'

'Nope. There's no jobs here.'

'Well, you'd need a new doorman for one. And you'd need to be able to climb down that ladder safely. Don't you think ahead?'

'Fuck me, Billy! You're a funny bloke, aren't you?' The owner was laughing now, starting to climb down the ladder. 'I can probably find something for you to do. Wear a white long-sleeve shirt and black tie. I'll see you at 8 p.m.'

I worked that door, nearly every night, for six years.

Brett was actually a really cool guy, and ever since that first bit of shit-shooting we got on really well. He paid $400 a week, which I couldn't believe. In the early nineties, that was a small fortune – our rent was only $75 a week, and everything else was cheap too. Suddenly we had the good life we'd always dreamed of, and we'd built it from scratch.

I loved Cairns. I remember that first day I arrived, there was this torrential rain coming down, a proper tropical storm. I looked up at the mountains, which were covered in banana trees, and they were all sort of bending over from the rain and the wind. Then the sun came out and they all dried out, sprang right back up again. It was an incredible sight, and it seemed like a lucky omen to me.

If I'd gone a little closer and checked out those banana trees, I would have seen that they were infested with spiders as big as your head. Maybe I wouldn't have thought that quite so lucky, although I don't mind spiders. They've got snakes up there big enough to swallow a small kangaroo whole, but they don't bother me either. At least they're honest. I've met some people in life who could learn a thing or two from snakes.

Cairns was a bit like the Wild West back then. It was rough – fuck, it was rough. But at the same time, it was very transient. People came and went: backpackers, hippies, FIFO workers. You'd see a face two or three times and then they were out of your life. If you had trouble with someone one night, the next day they'd be fucked off on a cruise or into the jungle, and you'd never see them again.

It was a lot of fun. Just like the old-timer on the Gold Coast had promised me, the Playpen was one of the best nightclubs in Australia. Most nights we had a couple of celebrities in, and every night I'd be surrounded by the prettiest girls in Cairns – models and actors up there on shoots, backpackers from all over the world in tiny outfits, looking for adventure.

The first time Lara came to see me at work, she was not impressed with all the pretty young things who'd flirt with the guys on the door. But she knew I wasn't about to do the dirty on her. We've always had a lot of trust in each other. We met when we were sixteen, and that was it for us. She's my best friend and the love of my life. I'm not going to do anything to hurt her. I mean, I'm not saying I didn't enjoy the attention back then, it was good for the appetite, but I always went home to eat.

If one wonderful woman isn't enough for you, I'm not one to judge. But Lara's all I ever wanted. After more than three decades together, I'm pretty sure she's a keeper.

21

Home improvement

Most people are afraid to die. I've never met someone at the end of their life who isn't devastated by the knowledge that they are about to die. Even the very religious ones, the ones who are 100 per cent certain they are about to live in God's Kingdom forever, don't want to leave the world and their families behind.

But not Terry. He didn't want to die, but he wasn't afraid either. Not an ounce of fear of death about the man, none at all. He would have liked to live longer, sure, but he was eighty-eight years old, and he'd lived exactly the life he'd wanted to. No regrets at all.

He'd married and raised a family with a loving wife, but she had died young. Terry never remarried, but he did go on to live a whole other life on top of that first one. He was leaving behind a whole brood of kids and grandkids, and having lived a hugely adventurous life he'd done everything on the planet he'd wanted to do.

Now that the end was in sight, there was just one thing he was absolutely terrified of, which is why he called me.

'There's some stuff in my house I need you to get rid of,' he told me. 'Nothing illegal, it's just private. But if the family finds it, they're going to put me in a fucking unmarked grave.'

Terry lived in a big country town in the Northern Rivers region of New South Wales. In the prime of his life he'd been your classic eighties bloke – fast life, fast money in a clip. White shoes and a coloured shirt unbuttoned down to the navel. He'd stayed that way all through his life, up until he was nearly ninety. But recently he'd had a fall and was taken to hospital, and once he'd been admitted it became clear that he wasn't going back home.

He'd been moved from the local hospital to a bigger one, up in Tweed Heads, where he was living out the last of his days. Even on his deathbed he was still the life of the party, incredibly playful and outgoing. He had quickly become best friends with his palliative care nurse, who'd heard about me through staffroom gossip and was the one who called me in to help settle Terry's affairs.

The clock was ticking, because his children were on the way to visit from interstate. He was so shit-scared, he would have broken both hips and given himself a heart attack just to get home and get rid of whatever this stuff was.

As far as he knew, his kids thought he was just a sweet old man. But it turned out that, until *very* recently, Terry had enjoyed what we might call an active social life.

'Viagra is the best thing that's ever happened to me,' he told me at our first meeting. 'Maybe to the human race.'

That's the kind of guy he was – completely out there.

At first I didn't like the bloke, to be completely honest. He told me that what he wanted me to get rid of were things of a sexual nature. My immediate thought was that this dirty old creep had a stash of kiddie porn, but he assured me it wasn't like that. He just had some very personal items he was absolutely petrified of his family stumbling upon.

I asked him to explain, and he started going into it, and after a couple of hours of hearing this bloke's stories I couldn't help but like him.

Terry had been a ladies' man – and a men's man. He'd dabbled in every kind of sexual experimentation you could think of and then some.

After retirement, he'd decided being a lonely widower wasn't for him, and he'd taught himself how to use the internet. He'd become very savvy with Craigslist and those sorts of websites. A world he'd never imagined but always wanted suddenly opened up to him. There he was, this older man with his bright pink shirt unbuttoned, tapping away at his keyboard, blown away by what he found.

'All my life I'd been interested in this and that,' he told me. 'But I never thought that I'd find someone who shared my interests. Or that I'd be inundated with younger women; all these 40-year-old women who wanted to meet an experienced older man who was into the same stuff they were.'

Even now, on his deathbed, you could see how amazed and grateful he was for the world he found online. Absolutely wide-eyed with wonder that all this kinky stuff he'd grown up thinking was weird and wrong was perfectly normal. No matter what you're into, chances are there's someone else out there who's into it.

He had no regrets, but he still didn't need his kids to know about what he liked to get up to in the bedroom with his harem of younger men and women. He needed me to go to his house, retrieve the items, incinerate them, and return with proof. He didn't give me an itemised list. Instead, he told me there was a room at the back of the house that would need a special key.

'Alright. So, what can I expect to find there?'

'Just your everyday sex-shop kind of things,' he said. 'And some things that are more . . . confronting.'

* * *

Terry's place, when I reached it, had nothing remarkable about it. A little split-level from the seventies, in red brick, on a street of similar houses. As I pulled up, Terry's neighbour, a middle-aged lady, approached me and asked if I was one of Terry's sons, and how he was doing.

I kept it vague.

'He's doing well,' I told her. 'He's in good spirits and he hopes to be home sooner rather than later.'

She seemed relieved, and very concerned for Terry's wellbeing, so I asked her if she wouldn't mind keeping an eye on the place until she heard from Terry – scare off burglars, water the plants, that sort of thing. She said she'd be very happy to do so.

I let myself in with the keys Terry had given me, deactivated the fairly serious home-security system, and made a quick search of the house. Again, absolutely nothing out of the ordinary. It could have been the home of any retired gentleman with a few dollars. Big TV in the lounge room, nice sofa.

Parts of the place looked exactly like the house from *The Partridge Family*, but the back half of the house was more modern than the rest – at some point a renovation had built another suite of bedrooms onto the back of the house.

I made my way back there and down the stairs, to a corridor that ended in a plain door with a complicated lock. Here it was. Terry had told me I would find the key hidden under the kitchen sink, behind a can of fly-spray, and sure enough it had been there: a single key, dangling from a novelty key-ring figurine of a naked woman.

I opened the lock, swung the door open, and stepped through into another world.

This was my first time in a sex dungeon. I've got to say, it was very nice. Not what I was expecting at all. If someone had asked me to picture an old man's sex dungeon, I'd probably have imagined something pretty sinister – black walls, no lights, dingy and disgusting. This was nothing like that – a very tastefully made room. It was all spotlessly clean. There was not a speck of dust on any of the many, many dildos.

The walls were done in a lovely pastel colour, and tasteful mood lighting from droplights illuminated different features. It was immaculate.

Terry had renovated the room all by himself, and he'd done amazing work. The D-rings on the wall, for attaching handcuffs, were sunk deep into the brick without cracking or stressing the plaster. Terry could have been an awesome builder in another life. I stood there, picturing this sweet old man going into Bunnings and asking the guys in the green aprons where he could find the ropes and chains.

Those chains were strung through with fairy lights, so at first glance they looked like ornamental lighting of the sort you'd find in a trendy cafe. I was looking at them, thinking, *Oh, that's pretty nice, what a good idea, maybe I'll do that in the living room,* for a solid minute before I realised what was going on.

In fact, everything in the room was sort of half-disguised to look innocuous. I picked up what I thought was a lamp, and it wasn't until I found the switch that I realised it was actually a vibrator.

The whole thing was designed in such a way that if one of Terry's kids had happened to stumble upon the room, at first glance they might just think it was some retirement reno project. You know – *Oh shit, Dad's losing his mind, he's put a fucking swing in the middle of the bedroom.*

This was my first encounter with a sex swing; I've never spent much time in swingers clubs or been into BDSM, so I was standing there scratching my head for ages, trying to figure out what this big fucking device hanging from the ceiling was supposed to be. Where you were supposed to put your feet, or your hands, or your whatever.

My next thought was, *How the fuck do I get this thing out of here?*

I could unscrew the swing from the brackets it was installed on, but after that, it was all in one big solid piece. It didn't fold up, and it was as substantial and heavy as a tire-swing you'd hang from a tree in your backyard. How was I supposed to get it down the driveway and into my car discreetly?

When I'd taken on the job, I thought I'd be dealing with a few dirty magazines, maybe a sex toy or two. Nothing I couldn't fit into a suitcase.

The sheer amount of sex toys boggled my mind. Not just dildos and vibrators and whatnot, but latex clothes, masks, chains, handcuffs, ankle cuffs, lubricants, body butters, oils and candles. I thought of putting everything in garbage bags, but that's not a good look – some stranger hauling loads of pointy objects out of a sick man's house in garbage bags.

In the end, I hit upon the idea of taking large sheets I found in a laundry cupboard and bundling the items up in those. In all, the sex toys amounted to three huge parcels, tied off at the top.

If the neighbour I'd met outside was still watching, she'd see me sweating as I hauled these huge sacks full of sex toys to my car. I must have looked like Santa for perverts – on my way to deliver treats to all the boys and girls who had been very naughty that year.

It made me wonder – the neighbour seemed like a lovely sort of a lady, and she was clearly very fond of Terry. How many times had she sat at his kitchen table for a nice cup of tea and a chat, not realising that she was metres away from one of the most well-appointed sex dungeons in Australia.

Then again, maybe she knew all about it and that's why she was so fond of Terry? You never know.

Before I left, I noticed the mailbox was packed with mail, so I collected it to deliver to Terry on completion of the job. I figured we were friends now, so why not?

Back home, I fired up the incinerator and used my phone to film myself destroying each item, one by one. It felt a little bittersweet, actually, watching these items that had brought so much joy to Terry's life consigned to the fire. You know that scene from *Star Wars*, where Darth Vader's helmet melts and the sad music plays? Imagine that, but with a big black sex swing.

* * *

The next day, I visited Terry and showed him the proof that his secrets had gone to the grave ahead of him. He was overjoyed, and very thankful that he could rest easy now.

He told me that his son had just arrived in town and was planning to let himself into Terry's house, staying the night in the spare bedroom. When he got there, he would find a nice suburban house, with friendly neighbours. Chances are he'd never think twice about the empty room with the bright pastel walls at the back of the house.

But who would? I guess the lesson is never underestimate your loved ones while they're still around. They're probably more interesting people than you think.

22

Playpen International

As the only venue in Cairns that could hold over 2500 people, the Playpen International was usually busy every night. And busy meant fighting.

On my first night, one of the other bouncers asked me if I'd brought a mouth guard. I thought that was ridiculous. Who the fuck wears a mouth guard to work the door of a nightclub? By the third night I was carrying two, just in case the first one was driven down my throat by a banana farmer who'd had a skinful.

Some nights were raw – just incredibly rough. I'd be ejecting one guy who'd been causing trouble and someone else would start up. Young blokes got too drunk and started fighting, breaking glasses, disrespecting women, and then it was battle stations.

Some people were just into fighting. Rough blokes who got off on violence and would go to a nightclub just to punch on with the bouncer. That was fine with me, though: I was one of them.

* * *

The truth is, I really enjoyed fighting. Not just punching people, but being punched. They say that's how you know you've got a problem with gambling – you start to enjoy losing just as much as winning. But that's how I related to pain. I loved the feeling of being hurt, because that was one of the few times in life I actually felt something.

Therapy in later life has made me realise that I learned to enjoy pain as a coping mechanism, because growing up the only attention I had from my mum was when she beat me. How sick is that? I'd see Mum getting out the kettle cord to whip me, and part of me would be like, *Well, she loves me enough to hurt me*.

I had this capacity to absorb tremendous amounts of pain, and not just to shrug it off but to appreciate it. Someone would sucker punch me and break my nose, and I'd sit there on the ground like, *That was a good punch. Excellent follow-through. Really got your shoulder into it. Well done.*

Then I would get to my feet and break them to pieces.

To stop me, you really had to do some damage – break some bones, take an eye out – or I wasn't going to stop coming for you. I just enjoyed it too much.

Don't get me wrong, I've been beaten up lots of times, but I had fun doing it.

There have been times I've picked myself up from the ground and been like, *Fuck, how'd I get down here?*

Someone would come up to me and say, 'Mate, you got elbowed in the face so hard we thought you were dead. Are you alright?'

My teeth would be all over the place, blood running down my throat, and go, 'I feel fantastic. Let's go again.'

* * *

At the Playpen, if someone walked up to the door and asked who wanted to fight, I'd be like a puppy dog that had been offered a walk.

'YEAH! ME! I wanna fight! Let's go!'

That would make them think again. 'Nah, you're just sick, fuck off.'

Then I'd be disappointed. 'Oh, are you sure? Try punching me a couple of times. Break my nose, see if you like it.'

The boss used to love it. 'You're so fucking sick in the head, they won't even fight you.'

He'd be packing up the club at 6 a.m. and he'd be delighted that there had been no trouble on the door. 'You're good for business, Bill. If nobody wants to fight, there's no incidents, no cops, no drama, no worries. You've got a job here for life.'

Any arsehole can finish a fight with his fists. It's a different set of skills to be able to de-escalate a situation. Luckily, I've always had the gift of the gab, and on the streets I learned to talk myself into – and out of – all sorts of problems. It's gotten me out of more trouble than I care to remember.

* * *

Through that job, I met some great people from all walks of life, from professionals in suits to policemen to railway workers.

I also got to meet all the bands that came through town. Any touring artist who could pull a crowd performed at the Playpen when they came to Cairns, and I ran security for them. I met The Angels, Hoodoo Gurus, Air Supply, Crowded House, Ross Wilson and Silverchair, just to name a few.

Most of them were great fun, although some of them were a bit full of themselves. There was one rock band frontman in particular who was a real prick. This guy was really arrogant and rude to everyone he considered beneath him, which was basically all the nightclub staff except for the owner. He was there to perform at a charity fundraiser for drug addiction amongst youth, and there he was, backstage, doing lines of coke and ordering everyone around. I won't name him, but he was a real angry little prick.

Jimmy Barnes was the complete opposite. A total gentleman, he was well mannered and friendly to everyone. Didn't have a problem with anything backstage, or if he did, he didn't let us know. He was happy just to be doing his thing. He was very curt and businesslike before the show, but not in a rude way, just a professional.

Jimmy was probably the best frontman I've ever seen work a room. He turned 3000 screaming people into a choir, every single person singing along with him. The room was overpacked and security were primed, ready for a big night – but watching Jimmy Barnes, there was no aggro at all. It's probably the only night in the history of Cairns nightlife without a single fight. The only person asked to leave was a drunk roadie harassing one of the bar girls; Jimmy later reprimanded him himself. The guy is a legend for a reason.

* * *

One Friday night in the middle of the nineties, I was standing on the door of the Playpen when this bloke turned up in thongs. Good-looking, he seemed nice enough, but we had a strict dress code that called for closed-toe shoes at all times.

'Not in those shoes, mate,' I told him. He just sort of blinked at me.

'Really?' he said.

'It's for your own good – there's broken glass all over the floor in there,' I said. I explained that if he went home and got changed into something smarter, I'd be happy to let him in for free. This was my way of showing patrons that not all bouncers are bad, and that I was trying to make their evening as pleasant and safe as possible.

Still, this bloke just stared at me.

'Maybe you should take a closer look at who you're talking to?' he suggested.

I didn't know who he was, and I didn't care much for his attitude. He seemed vaguely familiar, and I thought maybe he was some cocky backpacker I'd run into on the door previously.

I'd just moved him aside and was letting in the person behind him in line when a girl came up and asked for this bloke's autograph. Suddenly it struck me who he was: it was Val Kilmer, one of the biggest movie stars in the world. He was in town filming *The Island of Dr. Moreau*. I'd just knocked back Batman from the Playpen for wearing thongs.

I turned to Val and told him that, since I'd already let another guy in wearing thongs that day, I would let it slide this time. Of course, there was no guy.

I escorted him into the club, and notified the other security guys to look after him and see that he got a couple of extra drinks.

Rumours spread quickly in a town like Cairns, and as word got out that Kilmer was at the Playpen, people swarmed the place.

We ended up having one of the busiest nights of the year. When he left, he shook my hand and thanked me for my kindness.

After a few months of regularly hosting Val Kilmer and the rest of the cast and crew on *Dr. Moreau*, I was invited to a breakfast on set. That was fantastic, getting a look behind the curtain of a Hollywood production – all these beautiful people running about, this intense energy crackling in the air.

I was talking to a group of crew members about the film, which was apparently already going badly awry, when someone else came up to the group really excited.

'Marlon's here,' he whispered. 'Marlon Brando's on set.'

I was stoked. Marlon Brando is an actor of iconic status – the man, the legend, the all-around tough guy. I grew up watching the classic movies he was in, and every young man in the sixties and seventies wanted to be just like him.

I hung around on set for hours, hoping to meet the guy, but there was no sign of him. When it was time for me to go, I headed for the exit, disappointed.

On my way out, I passed an old man sitting in a wheelchair, this grumpy little island of stillness in a sea of people running in every direction.

'Good morning,' he grunted. He said something else, but his speech was so muffled I couldn't make it out.

'Good morning,' I said, politely, not wanting to be rude to an elderly gentleman. 'Gonna be a hot one. The humidity's gonna be shocking.'

This seemed to make the man even more depressed, and he muttered something else I couldn't make out.

'Okay, see ya!' I said, and went outside.

As I was leaving, a young man from the crew, who often visited the nightclub, came up to me and asked, 'What did he say?'

'Who?'

'Marlon Brando, who else?'

'How the fuck would I know?'

'You just spoke to him, Billy. That's him sitting right there.'

I was shocked, not because I'd just spoken to Marlon Brando, but because he was so . . . old. I was expecting the man from the movies – larger than life, strong, athletic, powerful. It was a bit confronting to meet this overweight, grumpy old man who was complaining about the weather.

Despite that, it occurred to me that everyone on set was steering clear of him out of respect for his status, and the heroic figure he'd once been. But I was delighted to have at least been polite to a legend, and that he took the time to say hello to me first.

I guess the lesson there is to never judge a book by its cover.

* * *

I started to get a reputation as a guy who knew how to watch someone's back professionally and discreetly, so people began approaching me with other security work. Off the back of looking after Silverchair, I was handpicked to assist with their concert in Kuranda, to the west of Cairns.

In turn, that led to private security work, which landed me in some pretty unique and interesting situations.

One highlight was working as Ken Done's bodyguard when he opened his first northern Queensland art gallery, keeping a wide berth around the homeless drunks who were hassling strangers on the street.

Probably the most memorable assignment was being part of a team selected to assist with the security of Bill and Hillary Clinton, and their advisors. A pretty remarkable example of how far I'd come – less than a decade earlier I'd been in solitary confinement in Boggo Road; now I was working alongside the secret service while President Clinton worked the room.

I still have a book of matches from the president's plane.

23

Confession

Nearly everybody who's hired me to interrupt their funeral service does so because of something they've left unsaid. Most of the time it's a secret – something they are ashamed of, or never had the courage to say. A few confessions haven't been secrets at all, just expressions of regret or sorrow that the deceased had never found the right words for before.

It's a real shame. Sometimes I stand up at a service and unfold that letter, and it becomes clear to me – and to everyone else in the room – how different things might have been if they'd just had the guts to share a few home truths during their life.

John Scott was a fun-loving guy. To give you an idea of the bloke, he had a custom coffin made out of a surfboard, with stylised waves rising up so that it looked like he was just taking a nap out on his board. He was a character, a larrikin – and a gambler, a drunk, a cheat and a liar. None of this was news to his girlfriend, or to his ex-wife. He'd more or less hired me just to apologise to them at his funeral.

With envelope in hand, I stood up and excused myself.

'My name is Bill Edgar and I am the Coffin Confessor. John Scott has engaged my services to interrupt his funeral and read aloud the following.

'If you're hearing this then I must be dead. First, thank you to those that made the effort to attend my funeral. To my girl-friend, Sally, I love you so much and wish we could have grown old together. But fate played a card we never saw coming. Please continue to remember me. I'll never forget you. Love always, Johnny.

'To my former wife, Sue, I'm sorry I hurt you. I'm sorry for all the pain and suffering, the lies, the guilt, the drinking and the gambling. I could have been a better husband, but I wasn't, and for that I am truly sorry. Please forgive me. Sue, you have found a good man in Jimmy, and you deserve to be treated like a lady. I can only hope the two of you live a full and happy life. By the way, does everyone here know you're pregnant? Or is that meant to be a secret? Have fun now.

'I engaged the Coffin Confessor, not to do my eulogy but to tell you all that I love you and that no matter what, I tried to be the best I could, even when I was being the worst. Take care, and please do me one favour: really live your lives.'

And that was that. He'd paid me a small fortune to express his sorrow and remorse for how he'd treated the women who'd loved him. Particularly his ex-wife; I think he'd shared a very deep bond of love with her.

Fair enough, it's not my place to judge – but at the same time, whenever I'm confronted with a case like that, I can't help but think how different things might have been for everyone if my client had gone out of their way to make amends before their time was up.

* * *

Then again, you've got people with no secrets, who just want a way to leave the world on their own terms. Jan Holden was definitely in that category.

Jan was an individualist – very much a sixties, earthmother sort of a woman. Into doing tarot readings and cleansing auras and that alternative, hippy counterculture type of life. There'd been a bloke in the picture at some point, as she had a daughter, but she lived with a woman that she'd been in a relationship with for most of her life.

They lived in an old Queenslander, one of those rickety wooden houses on stilts that look like they've had one drink too many and need to lean against the bar for a bit of a nap. Jan and her partner, Barbara, kept all the doors open, so when the breeze blew through the house, the polished glass wind chimes they'd hung in every room jingled in unison.

It was a happy home. There was no secret, no trauma that Jan wanted unearthed. She had some regrets, sure, but nothing that most of us don't accrue naturally over a lifetime.

Jan and Barbara had spent years saving for the trip of a lifetime, but they'd put off that dream holiday year after year until they could find the time. Then, when Jan finally retired, she got sick. The trip was off the cards. Now it would never happen.

Jan had accepted her imminent death as well as anyone I've seen. She hired me, I think, just to lift spirits at the funeral a little bit. She told me that she'd read an article about me and had asked her daughter to put things in motion, as she reckoned 'this would be a fun funeral'.

That's quite common, actually. I get a ton of requests for me to crash funerals in a particular outfit, or dressed up as a particular character. I get an inordinate number of requests to crash funerals dressed up as Homer Simpson. Why, I don't know. I don't really look in the mirror and see Homer staring back at me.

Someone else once asked me to dress up as Ricky Gervais. Weird.

I turn down those requests, but I was happy to accommodate Jan by interrupting her service.

We were standing around the gravesite, at Ipswich General Cemetery, watching the coffin being lowered into the ground, when I interrupted the sombre mood with the following.

'Please excuse me. My name's Bill Edgar and I am the Coffin Confessor. Jan has engaged me to interrupt her funeral service at this precise time. She has left some things unsaid, and thus I will read the following.

'Susan, my beautiful daughter, I'll be forever in your heart. Please become the person you want to be, and don't let anyone say you can't, because you can. I've left you everything I have. Do with it what you will, but remember you are woman, you are strong. I love you. Now spread your wings, baby girl.

'Barbara, my one true friend and lover, I wish we could have done this together. Please accept this gift: enjoy the trip of a lifetime. Think of me often, and know I'll be with you. Thank you for a wonderful life, filled with joy and love. Remember me and know that life is precious. Don't waste a minute of it. Make the most of what you've got.'

That was the message, as true as it was simple. Make the most of life.

And when it's time to move on, it's time to move on.

24

PI 007

After nearly eight years in Cairns, I began to feel I had outgrown it. The appeal of going toe to toe in fistfights with drunken farmers every night began to wane. My kids were growing up, and I was calming down.

We moved back down to the Gold Coast. I started a business in tree-lopping and later expanded into water-tank sales and installation. Unfortunately, the jobs began to slow, so I had to look for work elsewhere.

I applied for and was given a job as a debt collector in a call centre. I was fucking good at it. Before long I was pulling in huge sums of money for the company. Such enormous sums of money that I could hardly believe they were going to this shitty little debt collection agency.

It wasn't very inspiring work. I spent all day calling people up and leaning on them for not making payments on their debt. If, before I started the job, I thought that the job would be a good fit – some sort of bounty-hunter, tracking down dodgy types who had skipped out on loans – those illusions were shattered pretty quickly.

It was a job any moron could do. For six months, I watched as the company manipulated, coerced, deceived and otherwise used thuggish standover tactics to force vulnerable people to service debts they had no chance of paying off. In some cases, people hadn't even known they'd incurred the debt – it was some small fine or whatever, but it had quietly grown into this fucking monster debt without them being aware.

Then, in the course of investigating a debt, I stumbled over just how much money the company was making on each debt.

Debt collection companies purchase a bunch of outstanding debts from a lender, such as a bank, for a price below the value of the debt. Then, if they can get that person to pay it in full, they keep all that money and make a tidy profit. Except that these agencies buy many debts at once – they pay barely anything in the first place. When you break down the value of each debt compared to what it cost the agency, it's insane. Sometimes they pay less than $14 to cash in on a $50,000 debt.

For their part, the banks are insured. After passing a debt on to a collection agency, they can write it off. That's why they can afford to sell them for next to nothing.

Once they're in charge, the debt collection agency cranks up the interest on the money that's owed, much more than the banks would. And that's how they ruin your life.

It blew my mind. In my opinion, the way this system is rigged against ordinary people is nothing short of criminal. Of course, it's not illegal, although the debt collection industry would probably freely admit that it is immoral.

I finally had enough of that job when a woman being pursued by our agency took her own life. She owed a sum of money, and had grown more and more distressed about it as time went on. No doubt she had other problems in her life that contributed to her death, but being harassed by debt collectors just piles misery on top of misery.

It might not have been us that drove her to the brink, but I sure didn't feel good about it. I went to my bosses and told them that I believed we'd contributed to this tragic event. They told me to forget about it. When I pushed back, they told me that if I looked into it any further, they were going to have to terminate my role.

'Are you serious? Fuck that.'

I decided to quit, then jumped to the other side of the fence and took the fight to these agencies. I started to look into the underbelly of the industry, and started my own business, called Freedom from Debt Collectors.

Using what I knew from the other side of things, I taught people their legal rights and loopholes they could use to free themselves from unfair debts. The debt collection industry tried to bully me out of it, saying it was 'immoral'.

I was like, *You should know all about that*, and kept right on showing people how to avoid debt collectors.

In the course of looking into the mechanics of the industry, I realised I couldn't actually find all the information I needed. To bring about change in the industry, I would need a qualification behind me that offered some legal protections. Specifically, a private investigator's licence.

One government-approved PI licence course later – just some legal education and a tick-and-flick exam – and I was officially a private investigator.

* * *

It turned out being a PI wasn't nearly as exciting as it looked in the movies.

After getting your licence, the first couple of thousand hours on the job are for insurance companies. Say someone's made a claim after a public liability incident or a workplace accident, and they're due a payout – for big insurance companies, it's standard practice to bring in a PI to find fault with that claim, so they can refuse the payment or at least settle for a lower amount.

For example, a warehouse worker might claim workplace compensation for damaging his back on the job. The insurer will then pay someone like me to wait outside the worker's house until they can get photos of him doing something his injury should prevent, like mowing the lawn or carrying in his groceries. Less scrupulous investigators won't care if the evidence they turn over to the insurer is legitimate, circumstantial, or pretty much faked.

Once I had enough experience, I decided not to be involved in that side of the industry anymore. Instead I set up my own PI business, under my own name. It was as easy as placing an advertisement in the paper – the jobs started to roll in right away.

Most of the people who got in touch were husbands or wives who thought their partner was having an affair. Of course, they usually were. Time and time again I've seen it; if your relationship is in bad enough shape that you're hiring a stranger to investigate it, then photographic proof of your fears isn't going to fix the problem.

I spent more than a year following one guy, a prominent businessman who I nicknamed the Pigeon – a big stout guy with little legs, always strutting about. His wife contacted me, told me she suspected him of infidelity, and asked me to tail him. I told her it would be $150 an hour, which she readily agreed to. She was distraught, and money seemed to be no object.

The first day, I followed the Pigeon from business to business as he was making his daily deliveries. After about two hours I followed him into a suburban neighbourhood, where he pulled into the drive of a modern, low-set home and drove directly into the open garage. The garage door rolled down immediately after he entered, so I parked around the corner, out of sight but close enough for me to take surveillance shots from my car.

After forty minutes, the garage door creaked open again and the Pigeon's car reversed out. I snapped a roll of photos and figured I had evidence to bring to his wife – it had only been a few hours; this job seemed too easy.

I called my client and explained what had taken place. After a thoughtful pause, she asked me to stake the place out again the next morning. I agreed, and the next morning I parked around the corner from the mistress's house and waited. Sure enough, as regular as clockwork, the Pigeon rolled on into the garage.

I rang my client. She asked me if it was possible to get a shot of what was going on inside the house. That wouldn't be easy, this being a quiet suburb at 8 a.m., but not impossible.

I approached a neighbouring house and knocked on the door. A young woman answered and asked what I wanted.

'I live in the house behind yours. I'm thinking of putting it on the market.'

I asked if she minded if I ducked into her backyard to take some photos for the listing. She was very happy to let me do this, and left me to my own devices while I hung out in her yard and took shots of what was going on inside the Pigeon's cubbyhouse.

When I developed the photos, they revealed a woman in her fifties, wearing make-up and lingerie, sitting next to the Pigeon, who was eating a bacon and egg breakfast. He was wearing only a singlet and underwear. It was a cosy little post-coital scene, and surely everything my client needed to initiate a divorce.

We met in a cafe, and I gave her the photos. She flicked through them, growing very upset – she instantly recognised the woman in the pictures as her good friend and tennis partner. She began to cry, and I waited respectfully for her to process what she'd learned.

Eventually, she regained her composure. Wiping away tears, she said something unexpected. 'I want you to follow him for another two weeks. Can you do that?'

This surprised me, I must say. Gently, I reminded her that this was costing her $150 an hour, and she already had proof of her husband's infidelity and the identity of his mistress. Was she sure?

She was sure.

The thing is, the Pigeon never changed his routine. After two weeks, I had fourteen sets of nearly identical photos of the Pigeon cavorting with his lover. But when I took them to my client, she insisted I continue working the case, growing upset whenever I indicated I thought that was a bad idea.

So I kept following the Pigeon, except I didn't really have to do any actual following – I knew his routine back to front by then. I'd just go to the house he kept for his mistress, snap my photos, and wait for him to leave.

In the end I followed this guy for fourteen months, every single day.

It was a crazy situation. His wife didn't leave him. Now and again, I'd run into the Pigeon and my client at the movies together, or at a restaurant, holding hands. She'd pretend not to see me, and then a few days later we'd meet and I'd give her more photos of her husband cheating on her.

To this day, I don't know what was going on behind the scenes. My wife thinks my client was scared to leave her husband, and lonely – that she had hired me as a kind of a friend, someone who would sit with her while she cried. Maybe that was the case.

It occurred to me that maybe she got off on it, that this might have been some strange kink. Weirder things have happened, especially on the Gold Coast. You never really know what someone else's marriage looks like from the inside. In my opinion, it's better not to know.

I will never know what was really going through my client's mind. In the end, I had to drop the case, because I'd charged the poor woman a fortune in fees. She never missed a payment, never complained about the cost. For her, it wasn't about the money, it was about knowing where her husband was every minute of the day. It wasn't healthy, and after a certain point it seemed indecent for me to take any more money from her. I let her know I couldn't work for her anymore and we went our separate ways.

Years later, I read in the newspaper that the Pigeon had died. Just dropped dead of a heart attack on the golf course. After that, the mistress came out of the woodwork. She sued for some of his assets, on the grounds that they'd been in a de facto relationship for an extended period of time. She got nothing – she didn't have any proof that they'd been together all that time. The ironic thing is, the wife did! Fourteen months of photographic evidence of her husband's love for his mistress.

* * *

I much preferred the industrial side of the PI work. Going undercover in businesses to find out who was responsible for theft or vandalism within an organisation.

One of the biggest clients for this kind of thing is the hotel industry, where theft is a major problem. They have a huge problem with wage fraud – people falsely claiming hours worked when they haven't actually turned up. It's rampant amongst the low-waged workers at hotels: cleaners, kitchen hands. They'll get a friend on staff to clock on with their timecard, so they can say they worked the shift when they didn't. Then some other day, they'll do the same thing for their friend.

Some places I've gone undercover in, you'll have one person running around with four other people's timecards. It might not seem like a big deal, but if hundreds of staff across a hotel chain are doing it, that adds up to millions of dollars each year.

One of my very first jobs in a hotel was for one of the large luxury hotels on the Gold Coast, where they asked me to sort out this kind of thing. I went in undercover as a security guard, which was easy enough given my background.

The manager went around and introduced me to all the staff, using my false identity, and from there I started to get the lie of the land.

On maybe my second night, I turned to the other boys in security and told them I was starving. 'Hey, any idea where I can get some food around here?'

The other guards didn't even blink. One of them told me exactly how to break into the kitchen fridges, encouraging me to take my pick of all the luxury high-end food in there.

'Try the salmon,' one of the guards said. 'It's delicious.'

'Don't take the salmon,' another guard chimed in. 'Or, if you do, make sure you take the whole thing. They'll get suspicious if there's half a salmon in the fridge.'

Apparently, every other night this guy went home with a whole salmon under his coat.

I couldn't believe it. It hardly seemed necessary to go undercover – they just leapt at the opportunity to incriminate themselves. The whole hotel was rotting from the inside. Inventory shrinkage, theft, wage theft, vandalism by disgruntled employees. The perpetrators weren't shy about it; they made themselves known to me.

When I had everything I needed, I was out of there. One night I just acted like I'd cracked the shits with management and walked off the job. 'This place is fucked,' I told the other staff. 'I'm outta here. See ya.'

As far as they were concerned, I was just another unhappy security guard. There was very little chance they'd join the dots when, a couple of weeks later, they were called into the manager's office.

I'm never around when management confront the staff who have gone rogue. You don't really need someone like me there for that. People are generally pretty keen to confess, once you put pressure on them. There's nothing quite as heavy to carry around as a guilty conscience.

25

Embarrassing items

Say you died right now – what if you put down this book, crossed the street and got collected by a bus? There would be a mess to clean up. Not just right there on the scene, although yes, it'd probably ruin the poor bus driver's day, but also in a more general sense. Someone – usually your partner, parent or child – is going to have to put your home in order. Actually, physically go through all your worldly possessions and put them into boxes and move them on to another location or throw them out.

Think about what's in your home, right now. Chances are there are bits and pieces lying around that you wouldn't want your next of kin coming across. What's it for you? A stash of dirty magazines in the back of the cupboard? Sex toys hidden under the bed?

Perhaps you have love letters from an old flame you've kept for sentimental reasons that you wouldn't want your spouse to find. Or maybe a folder of emails on your laptop chronicling the affair you've been having?

It doesn't have to be sexual. Maybe you're in debt, maybe you're a gambler. Maybe it's as innocent as a freezer full of microwave burritos when you were supposed to be watching your weight.

Everyone's ashamed of something. When your grandmother told you to always wear clean underwear in case you were hit by a bus, she wasn't just speaking literally. If you were to die, without warning, wouldn't you want someone to be able to take care of your dirty laundry?

Take Marcus. Top bloke, salt of the earth. Divorced, no kids. Days left to live.

He was a tradie, an electrician, and one day he had a bit of an accident on the job and sprained his elbow. *No worries*, he thought, and went to the hospital for a routine scan. There, they told him he had a rare type of cancer and didn't have long to live.

Until that moment, he hadn't felt sick at all, but suddenly he started to go downhill, fast. It's one of those things – once your mind has convinced your body that you're dying, it doesn't take long at all. It became clear very soon after his diagnosis that he was never going home from the hospital.

Now, Marcus had lived a good life. His marriage hadn't worked out, but he was leaving the world on pretty good terms – family that loved him, no enemies, no animosity. But he had been horny, as blokes can be. He was popular with the ladies, and now he had a computer back at his house with a few dozen dating profiles, message threads with all these different women.

No big deal, but Marcus was terrified that the women he had been seeing would feel disrespected by what was on his computer.

There was that, and a few other items lying around – basic sex toys, a vibrator, a butt plug. He had a brother who was coming to pack up his house for him, and he wanted that computer destroyed before anyone saw what was on it.

He'd actually called a friend of his, a police sergeant, and asked him to break in and take care of it. The sergeant explained that he couldn't do that, that it was illegal for police to enter a property without a warrant and take private property, even off duty. It makes sense – you don't want cops to have that sort of power without regulation.

'You need to call Billy,' the sergeant told him. 'He's a PI up on the Gold Coast, and he'll be able to help you out.'

Sure enough, I could help him. I'm well versed in the legal ramifications of my PI work: what I can and cannot do and stay within the bounds of the law. Entering private property to secure a client's privacy and peace of mind? No problem.

Helping Marcus out was actually the first post-mortem home sweep I conducted. As time passed, and word of the Coffin Confessor spread, I got more and more requests along these lines.

Some people didn't want anything hidden or destroyed – they just had items of particular value they wanted to be rescued and kept safe. Truth be told, when movers are engaged to help pack up a deceased estate, it's not uncommon for an item of value to vanish along the way. I reckon it's a special kind of fucked up to steal from someone on their deathbed, so I was always willing to help out in these scenarios.

Often people wanted me to secure computers, valuable documents or jewellery – the sort of thing that you'd expect a light-fingered chancer to steal. But other times they were purely objects of sentimental value – photos, letters, little mementos collected over the course of a lifetime.

One or two of these requests made no sense, even to me.

One lady – a very airy-fairy hippy – just wanted me to pick her car up and transport it, along with a number of items in the boot, to her brother's property. When I first popped the boot, I was expecting to see something that justified her hiring me for a not insignificant sum of money to keep this stuff safe. Jewels or gold bars, or bricks of heroin or something. But it was nothing like that, just a couple of boxes of household items – a PC, files, photo albums.

It was just that she distrusted the authorities and wanted to make sure her shit was secure. I doubted anyone was going to hijack the vehicle to steal her fucking crystals and wind chimes, but some people are just eccentric I guess, or paranoid.

Then again, some people have every reason to be paranoid.

26

The Lost Boy of TSS

Life has turned out pretty fantastic for me, in the end. I married my best friend, and together we've raised a family, made a home. I've built a career for myself on nothing but my wits, the gift of the gab and hard work.

Although you could reach the suburb I grew up in with a short drive, by the late nineties I was a million miles away from the hellish situation I'd been born into. Fate had dealt me a bad hand, but through sheer force of will I've made my life so good it would have been unrecognisable to the poor, frightened child I'd once been.

I did really fucking well. That might sound boastful, but that's only because I'm boasting. I'm proud of what I've achieved. It's incredible. I know a lot of privileged kids I went to TSS with who haven't come half as far despite starting way ahead of me.

But, since my second year at TSS, I've understood that it can be its own kind of curse to be born into that kind of privilege.

Protected from harm and failure by the mighty dollar, when some did fall over life's hurdles they took it harder than most.

The pressure that family and society put on privileged children is immense, and when they failed to reach the goals others had set for them, they struggled. For every success story TSS trumpeted in their alumni literature, there was another child who broke under the pressure and fell through the cracks.

What I didn't understand at the time is that some of those children had been struggling with the same demons I had. Like me, they had suffered sexual abuse at the hands of teachers at TSS.

* * *

In 1997, the news broke that TSS old boy and Rugby League legend Peter Jackson had died of a heroin overdose. After graduating, he'd become a police officer, then blossomed into a rising star on the rugby field. He'd played for Souths, then the Broncos, before representing Queensland and finally the Australian and English international teams.

But after he retired, he had a troubled few years. He passed away when he was only thirty-three.

Before he died, he confided to his wife that he'd been systematically sexually abused by his housemaster and coach at TSS, a former priest. The abuse started when he was fourteen and lasted for over a year. It had derailed poor Peter's life, and then ended it.

I was staggered. I'd known Peter back in the day. I had never actually met him at school, but befriended him at a drug dealer's house in the Gold Coast, back in the eighties. He was a great bloke, really friendly, outgoing and charming. I'd not for a second suspected he'd been abused.

Those reports in 1997 were the first time I knew there were other boys who'd been abused at TSS. And I understood that if there were two of us, then there must be more. Many more.

That gave me the strength to come forward myself. It wasn't a great feeling to think that there were others who'd suffered as I had, but at the same time it was good to know for sure that I wasn't alone. It took Peter Jackson's death to spur me into starting my crusade.

* * *

I wrote letters to the school with my allegations, asked for meetings, asked them to do something. They ignored me. The cops too.

I started searching for other boys who'd been abused at TSS, but it was impossible. Tracking people down was no problem for me, but getting them to speak about something that was so shameful, so taboo, that was a different matter. They'd been utterly indoctrinated into the culture of this prestigious school.

I had very little success until social media came along. When I went on Facebook and made a post about Peter, and about my own experience of abuse, a guy a year or two above me got in touch within two hours.

'Scott Robinson?' he said. 'Is your name Scott Robinson, from the Southport School?'

'It's Bill now, but I used to be called Scott.'

'Mate, you're an urban legend back at TSS. The kid who left and never came back. They call you "The Lost Boy".'

So I set up a Facebook page with my story: The Lost Boy of TSS. That's when the other boys started to come forward. One, then two, then a trickle, then a flood. Dozens of boys who'd been abused, going back decades.

One lady was seventy-four, and she told me that her brother had taken his own life after being sexually abused while at TSS.

From 1968 to 2016, we've counted 133 boys who have come forward.

Then there are all the boys who can't come forward, because they didn't survive long enough. We found at least eight boys who had taken their own lives since 1997. Many of those deaths were at the school itself. One boy stood in front of the school's clock tower and blew his brains out. Others climbed into the roof of the theatre and hung themselves from the rafters.

On official reports, each of the suicides is chalked up to poor mental health. You know what contributes to poor mental health? Suffering abuse at school! That's not a great practice to get into if you care about mental health.

Each of the boys from TSS who came forward had their own complex trauma and needed to talk about it. At the same time, I was getting inquiries from lawyers who were representing these men in reparation cases, seeking reports about their mental health. I told them that I could give them affidavits as a certified PI, but they really needed the perspective of a qualified counsellor.

I decided I needed to find some way to help. I looked into it and realised the way forward was for me to become a registered counsellor. I went to the relevant medical practitioner board, where I explained who I was and what I was trying to do. They spent two weeks deliberating, and then came back and told me they would cover my insurance in a self-regulatory capacity.

So it went from the Lost Boy of TSS to the Lost Boys of TSS. Plural. A community. We function as a support group for each other. That sort of solidarity is invaluable, particularly when standing up against the church.

I never believed in strength in numbers, but I do believe in the power of overwhelming evidence. The more of us who come forward, the less convincing TSS, the church, and all their feeble evasions and excuses become.

When I first started to actively pursue justice, TSS did everything they could to silence me. A school official called me and told me I would be taken to court for making false claims, and that I was a dishonest character with a grudge.

He learned pretty quickly that empty threats don't go a long way to persuading me. The following day he called to apologise, and asked if we could meet in private and discuss compensation for the harm caused.

A meeting with the principal revealed that my school file had been removed. He informed me that he could not be of much assistance, as my abuse had occurred before his time. He also indicated that a few old boys had come forward to him personally, and that the school had assisted them financially.

In time, I got a written apology and an offer for a small sum of money in exchange for my silence. My answer was a resounding 'Fuck no.'

I don't want their money. Newspapers reported that Peter Jackson's widow got $250,000. What is that, for a life? It's fuck all. That's not what I want. I want them to dismantle the system that harboured child abusers and failed vulnerable children.

In 2017, I found Mr X, the teacher who'd digitally raped and molested me in his office, was still teaching at another school. The Queensland police were alerted, but that was the last I ever heard of it. No contact was ever forthcoming about my complaint. That's not the outcome you get when a school is serious about repairing the damage they've done.

* * *

The message I'd like to get across is this: you can't give up. If you've been abused, you can't ever give up.

If you've never dealt with what happened to you, if your life's in turmoil, you've got to get off the fence. I know it's the hardest thing of all, but you've got to accept that it happened. Because you can go a lifetime without confronting it. You can take drugs, drink, or just repress it and keep it in a bubble – until you break down entirely.

That's sure as shit what I did.

Because that bubble can't hold forever. And when it does burst, you end up in a shitload of pain. It'll rot you away from the inside.

Once I learned to accept what had been done to me, I started to move on. A few people told me, 'It fucking happened, deal with it, get over it.'

No. I won't get over it. But I *will* deal with it. I will *expose* it. Because the more I tell my story, the more it helps other people.

The most important thing I'd like to get across is that only you have the power to accept it. And that's a tremendous power. Because once you accept it, you can forgive yourself. Don't worry about forgiving anybody else – because you can't. You'll never forget what happened, but you must forgive yourself, because it wasn't your fault.

That's what us victims do – we always blame ourselves, for years. What did I do wrong? What choice did I make that made them think they could do this to me? Was I not strong enough, not good enough, not smart enough to keep myself safe?

That's all bullshit. Forgive yourself.

Because once you do, fuck – the power that it gives you, it's incredible. I've gotten so much power from it.

Nowadays, people hear my story and go, 'Oh, you poor little kid.'

Fuck you, I'm not a poor little kid. I was eight when it started and sixteen by the time it ended. I was a victim of predators and powerful institutions. Now I'm a man, *I* have the power.

Don't feel sorry for me. I'm not sitting in the gutter feeling sorry for myself; I have too much strength and courage for that shit.

Victims of abuse – sexual, physical or mental – can remain victims or they can become survivors. It's their choice, but I can honestly say the empowerment from deciding to be a survivor is like no other.

I'd encourage any victim to own it. Use it to better yourself. Don't sit in silence. Shout, kick and scream. Make a noise so loud that the people who hurt you hear it in their sleep. You'll save your own life, at a minimum, but chances are you'll be saving others from what you went through.

27

Sky daddy

Nobody wants to die. Even for very religious people, as their final hour approaches, there is doubt. You'll see them hanging on to their icons, praying. 'God is with me.' 'Soon I will walk in the Kingdom of Heaven.' 'The Lord is my shepherd.'

Fine, the Lord is your shepherd. But I've seen farms, mate. Being a sheep isn't all it's cracked up to be, and in fact, nor is being the shepherd.

Religion. It's not for me. I believe, when we die, we go to sleep and that's it. End of story. I don't think there's more to it than that, but it doesn't sound so bad to me. Maybe I'm wrong – I hope I am.

The way I see it, it's just another journey. You go to sleep and maybe you wake up, maybe you don't. Nobody knows for sure. Even the people who *do* know for sure – 100 per cent believe that they'll go to sleep in the ground and wake up on a cloud, surrounded by cake and puppies and angelic choirs – are shit-scared in their final days.

But what's on the other side of that fear? It could be joy, love, happiness, hellfire, torture, a million fucking things. You're not going to know for sure until it happens to you, so no amount of faith is going to stop you from feeling that mortal fear.

* * *

Dale Peters had no doubts. He hated religion, hated God and hated anything to do with either.

I'm not sure what had happened to Dale to make him so disgusted with the whole thing, but I don't think I've ever met anyone more staunchly opposed to the church. Even I don't hate it that much.

I mean, in my opinion they're a criminal organisation of thieves and paedophiles, but you can't deny that they've paid for some nice paintings and sculptures over the years. And don't forget they *do* feed the hungry, even if it's as a front for committing the most heinous of crimes.

Dale didn't want a fucking bar of it. The problem was that his family was deeply religious, and they wanted a proper Christian burial for their son. Their biggest fear was that if he didn't repent on his deathbed and have his burial presided over by a priest, he would burn in hell. That was fine by Dale. He didn't believe in hell, and so it wasn't much of a threat to him.

Dale's entire being was opposed to the idea of a religious funeral, but no matter how many times he told his family that the idea of being farewelled in a church was distressing to him, they wouldn't listen. The argument grew so bitter that, in his final days, when Dale could have really used the support of his family, they grew estranged. He was left to go through it more or less alone.

What do you do when your family abandons you in your hour of need? What option do you have when they insist on a religious funeral and that's literally the last thing in the world you want? How do you make sure your wishes are carried out? You fucking hire someone to do it. You give me a call.

'I'm pissed off,' he told me when we first met. 'And I'm scared.'

'You should be,' I said. 'I would be scared shitless.'

He laughed at that. 'Aren't you supposed to comfort me?'

'Where's the comfort? You're dying. It's not like I can say anything to change that. If you told me I was going to die today I'd shit myself too. I'm scared for you, because you're going before me. That's a bum fucking deal.'

He smiled. I think he respected the honesty, that I wasn't trying to sugar-coat things.

We agreed to work together, and he told me exactly what he wanted done. He was precise in his instructions, and he was angry. Full of rage towards the divide religion had created in his family. It was all 'fuck this', 'fuck that' and 'fuck them for putting me through this'.

I think part of what he needed was just to have someone to vent to. He was hurt pretty badly by the whole thing. The way he talked about God and religion, and the traditions he'd been brought up with, was really biting and actually very funny.

But most of all Dale was angry, scared, lonely, hurt. I helped him as best I could.

When he died, he left me with his final message.

* * *

The signal for me to interrupt Dale's funeral service was when the minister invited the assembled mourners to pray. Dale had been adamant about this: no prayer at his funeral.

I got to my feet and delivered Dale's final message.

'I'm speaking on behalf of my client, Dale Peters, and would like you to please shut up, sit down, and listen to what Dale has left unsaid.

'To those of you who organised this funeral service: this is not about you, it's about me and my wishes. Not yours. I didn't want a religious funeral. I'm a fucking atheist, for fuck's sake!

'I get it – you want to be seen by everyone in this room as doing the right thing. Well, the right thing would have been to support me while I was dying.

'Fuck it. You know you're all going to die, and time waits for no one. You can't buy more of it. I'll see you all when you get to the same place I am now.

'Finally, I'm pissed off, I'm upset and I'm angry. I didn't want to die. I didn't want to get sick and suffer. But most of all, I didn't want to find out the hard way who loved me and who didn't. You can all get fucked. Amen.'

I've got to say, after a moment of shocked silence, I was not warmly received by Dale's family.

It was very clear the room was divided into two halves. The family on the left, who were outraged, and Dale's friends on the right, who were loving it.

The anger from the family was real; you could feel it coming off them. There was a bit of shouting, a few threats. That's actually the first time while crashing a funeral that I felt like somebody might attack me physically. Those mild-mannered Christians were way scarier than the bikies.

I moved quickly to place the letter back in its envelope, put it on top of the coffin, and left.

I was in the car park when someone came out of the church, yelling for me to wait. I turned around, ready for a bit of trouble, and this young man came up to me.

'I'm Dale's best mate. You did the right thing back there. Don't listen to his family, they didn't really know him – he would have loved that.'

With that, I drove away, and Dale's mate went back into the service, to deal with the aftermath.

28

Fear time, not death

In my home office, there's an old-fashioned clock. It looks a bit like a grandfather clock, but the face of the clock is a silly picture of a cartoon cow.

The kids and I found this clock years ago, when I'd taken them out to buy a birthday present for Lara. They made money by doing chores around the house, and they'd saved up just over sixty dollars, so we were looking for something in that price range.

We were passing this old junk store and my daughter just zeroed in on this clock. She fell in love with it right away. It chimed while we were examining it, playing a happy little four-note melody, which only enchanted the kids more.

When I asked the shopkeeper what it cost, he thought about it for a moment.

'I'll give it to you for sixty bucks.'

'Deal,' I said.

Some things are just meant to be.

That clock is still going, ticking away. Every fifteen minutes the chime goes off, the same happy little melody. After a few years I couldn't even hear it anymore, it just became part of the background noise, like rain on the roof or the birds singing at sunrise.

And then one day I was just sitting on the couch after work and it dawned on me. I'd heard that tune before. It was the sound of the Big Ben chimes – the same melody that played every fifteen minutes at the Southport School.

This tune had soundtracked three of the worst years of my life. It played in the background while I was humiliated and abused.

You'd think I would hate that sound, but even after I recognised it, I really didn't feel one way or the other about it. It's just the chimes of a clock. It's not the teacher who groomed me, or the grandfather who molested me, or the mother who sold me out and then abandoned me. It's just a pretty tune, one that plays to let me know that the clock keeps ticking and the hours keep slipping away.

If anything, I find the tune relaxing now – it's a reminder that all that shit is in the past, that I'm never going to go through anything like that again.

If it's a reminder of the past, it's a reminder to never forget where I came from. And because of that, it's a reminder of how far I've come. I look around at home, at my family and this life we've built together, and I'm struck: *This is fucking awesome.*

And it is. Now that life is sweet, all things considered, I make sure I still take every day as it comes, the same way I did when I was starving on the street.

It's the days that are precious. The hours, the minutes. The clock doesn't mean a fucking thing, but it's a reminder that I fear time more than I fear death. Death comes for us all, but not all of us remember to make the most of the time we have. Out of everything I've learned along the way, that's the only hard and fast rule. Tick-tock.

29

Death don't wait

Just the other night, while I was at home with my family, Lara's brother, Scott, passed away in his sleep.

I had first met Scott thirty-five years earlier, when I was just sixteen. He was the one who chased me through the streets of Surfers Paradise to try to scare me off dating his little sister. That didn't work – not only did I keep dating her, I married her and she became the mother of our two children, and grandmother to three grandchildren.

But for three years in the eighties, I avoided Scott like my life depended on it, which I thought it did. He was huge – one of the biggest blokes I'd ever seen – and fast, too. I couldn't believe how fast he could run. I was faster, but I really had to work at it to escape him.

One day, he finally cornered me right out the front of Replay World, an arcade full of pinballs and pool tables.

There he was, looming over me, and then he just sort of shrugged.

'You know, I don't really remember why I was chasing you. Did you do something bad to my sister?'

'No, I love Lara. And she loves me.'

'Right. That's all good then,' he said, and went on his way.

He really was a good bloke. The definition of a gentle giant. He might have looked like he could crush you with his bare hands, but the closest I ever saw him come to violence was demolishing a bag of chips.

* * *

Scott and I became close as the years went by. We'd chat about my work as the Coffin Confessor, death and the afterlife. He was intrigued by the stories I told him about my clients, all the unique requests they made, what really mattered to them when it came down to the wire.

He told me he didn't really mind what sort of funeral he had, just as long as he was cremated. He didn't want to be buried in a coffin under any circumstance, because he had this morbid fear of being buried alive. That they'd think he was dead when he was really just in a coma, and then he'd wake up in the coffin. Silly, but the thought scared the shit out of him.

'When I die, I want you to stab me with a pin,' he told me. 'Get a big needle and jam it into my toe to make sure I'm really dead.'

'Sure.' I laughed. 'There would have been heaps of times back in the day when I would have been happy to stab you.'

'No, I'm serious. When I go, stick a pin in me. If there's any reaction, don't burn me.'

'Alright.' I agreed that if Scott passed away before me, the Coffin Confessor would turn up and make sure he was really gone.

When Scott did pass away, he was only fifty-seven. He was found on his sofa, in front of the TV, where he seemed to have passed away watching his shows. The coroner's report determined that Scott had died of natural causes, which did lead me to wonder what the fuck 'natural causes' means at fifty-seven. I later discovered that Scott had sought medical attention a few hours earlier and was given morphine for a headache.

I made sure Scott received his last wishes. As the Coffin Confessor, I went to the viewing, where a polite mortician in neat clothes showed me the casket where Scott's body was being prepared for cremation. The mortician stood in respectful silence, finally asking me if I'd like a moment alone with the deceased.

'I'll just need a second,' I said.

When the mortician was gone, I pulled out a needle. I plunged it into Scott, and then a second time, really deep. No blood, no bruising, no reaction.

At that moment, I was suddenly really sad. I realised part of me had been hoping that Scott's eccentric fear had been justified. That he would react, move a little, then spring up from the slab complaining of a headache.

'Alright, mate,' I said. 'Now you can be sure.'

I said my final goodbye to a man only a few people ever had the pleasure and privilege of knowing well.

* * *

After all that, I found myself in the strange position of giving a eulogy. A regular, respectful recounting of the sort of man Scott had been. No interruptions, no confrontations, no secrets to reveal.

Scott might be the only man in the world who didn't die with any secrets. All he'd wanted me to disclose was the love he had for his children, grandchildren, family and friends. I can honestly say I don't think I ever knew a guy who was so steadfastly loyal and loving to the people in his life. All he ever wanted was the best for his kids and peace for everyone around him.

The one little Coffin Confessor flourish he'd asked me to do was to call out the people who had wronged him over the years and let them know all was forgiven.

That was it. Fifty-seven years. A good life, a good man.

* * *

At home, after the funeral, I passed the arcade table I had purchased a few years earlier and thought of the time Scott cornered me in that Gold Coast pinball parlour, all those years ago.

The table was fully functional, but it was an antique – the sort of thing they used to have in every video arcade in the eighties. Just like the tall clock, I'd found it in a second-hand store and bought it on impulse.

When I was a kid, starving on the streets, I used to hang around pinball parlours, trying to stay out of the weather. I'd always desperately hope someone would invite me to play a round. To put a couple of coins into the machine to play a game was an unimaginable luxury to me back then – every penny had to go towards food.

Now, I'm good. I'll never be hungry again. If I wanted to, I could spend the rest of my life playing video games. But life's too short for that. I never actually play, but I like to keep the table, and think about what it represents. How far I've come, from that kid who had nothing to a man who has everything he ever wanted.

But in the end the arcade table, the clock, everything I own, they're just objects. Objects are impermanent – they're not coming with me when I die. They're nice to have for now, but I couldn't give a fuck about them in the long run. Motorbikes, bank accounts – just more bullshit, ultimately.

Trust me, when you're on your deathbed, you're not going to be stressing about your share portfolio. You're going to regret the things you never said, the things you never did, the opportunities you never took; whether out of fear or some misguided sense of propriety and social norms. None of that matters at the pointy end of a palliative care ward.

If you die today, you won't be worried that you missed out on a promotion at work, or that your childhood was terrible, or that you drive a shit-box car while your neighbour has something a little shinier. You'll regret that idle afternoon you spent wasting your finite time on earth worrying about bullshit. You'll regret not hugging your spouse and telling them you love them.

Think about it, when was the last time you took your significant other (spouse, boyfriend, girlfriend, polyamorous genderqueer pod-buddy – I don't give a fuck, as long as you give a fuck about them) out for a nice dinner and a movie? What are you doing that's more important than that?

The day Scott died, I realised that I know more people who are dead than alive. That's not a sad thought; it happens to all of us. It'll happen to you – if it hasn't already. As the years go on, more and more of the people I've loved will die, leaving me with more memories than people. Then, soon after that, I'll be dead, and those memories will die with me. And that's fine, that's natural.

As for what happens after you die, I'll take that the way I took life – as it comes, one day at a time. I don't believe in the afterlife, but I do believe in living, and I know that is the most important thing.

I knew Scott. I knew Michael. I know Lara, and my kids and grandkids, and those relationships are the only part of life that matters, in the end. When I die, they will have known me. And they'll know that I lived the only way I could, with never a backward step. And death is just another step forward.

If there is a God, well, I'm for hire. Maybe he'll ask me to do what he can't, won't, or is too afraid to do, just as those here on earth have done. If that doesn't work, then I guess I can apply for a job with Satan. I'm sure a position will open up. Whether it's for God or the devil, or both, there's always work to be done.

I don't mind what happens to my earthly remains. It's just a body, after all. Just another object. Crash my funeral if you like – I've got nothing to confess. Although maybe stick a pin in me before you throw me on the fire.

Acknowledgements

To my son, Joshua, thank you for your unconditional love, support and friendship.

To my daughter, Candis, thank you for believing in me and never allowing me to give up.

To Steve Mandell, Michael, Greg Page (former Yellow Wiggle), John McAvoy, Greg Haddrick, Doug and Brooke McCamley, Casper and the team at Penguin Random House Australia, thank you for believing in me, encouraging me and supporting me.

And, finally, to those no longer with us, who allowed me to tell those you loved how much you loved them, and those you loved to hate to f**k off, I thank you.